Books by Irma Rhode

PRACTICAL ENTERTAINING (1978)

COOL ENTERTAINING (1976)

PRACTICAL
ENTERTAINING

PRACTICAL ENTERTAINING

Irma Rhode

NEW YORK

Atheneum

1978

Library of Congress Cataloging in Publication Data
Rhode, Irma.
   Practical entertaining.
   Includes index.
    1. Entertaining. 2. Cookery. I. Title.
TX731.R47   1978   642'.41   78-53801
ISBN 0-689-10915-6

INTRODUCTION

I LOVE TO COOK and I love to entertain, but I will not be in the kitchen while my guests are in the living room having fun over cocktails, exchanging sweet gossip and discussing the latest political scandal. So, over the years, I have developed a number of recipes that do not require constant attention and can be finished in a few minutes. This of course takes careful planning, doing as much as possible before the guests arrive, going even so far as getting the water measured for frozen vegetables. I have a timetable worked out: when to put what in the oven, light a fire, turn off a fire, and so on. I do not use a timer—that would alert my guests to what I am up to—so I keep time with my watch. I try to give the impression that I wave a magic wand and the food marches out of the kitchen. Another thing I have learned over the years is that expensive food does not necessarily make for a successful dinner party. I have had more applause for poached meatballs than for the fanciest filet of beef.

This book is divided into three parts, covering three different situations a hostess may be faced with. The first part deals with meals that can be put together fast—the impromptu dinner. We all have had surprise telephone calls, issued a spontaneous dinner invitation and, after hanging up the receiver, realized that the larder was empty. So all the ingredients used in this section can be purchased at the supermarket at the last minute. These recipes are for four portions. The second part deals with meals that can be cooked the night before, with recipes for six portions. The third part deals with meals that are prepared leisurely during the day the dinner is to be served. They are my favorites, with a whole day to get ready! These recipes serve eight. Hors d'oeuvres recipes throughout the book are for twelve pieces, as that is an easy number to multiply or divide, depending on the number of guests and the variety of hors d'oeuvres on your menu. All the dishes have been served in my home many years, and for many years my friends have been asking for the recipes. I hope you will enjoy these meals as much as my guests have.

Irma Rhode

CONTENTS

PART THREE   *(Recipes for Eight)*

PART ONE

(ALL THE RECIPES ARE FOR FOUR)

PART ONE

HORS D'OEUVRES

SARDINES AND TOAST FINGERS

One 4⅜-ounce can boneless and skinless sardines
A few drops lemon juice
3 or 4 lemon wedges
2 slices of white toast

Drain sardines, place on a serving plate, and sprinkle with lemon juice. Arrange lemon wedges around the sardines. Cut each slice of toast into 6 fingers and arrange them around the lemon wedges. Let the guests help themselves.

HERRING TIDBITS

1 jar herring tidbits, or a can of gafelbiters
Butter
2 slices pumpernickel or whole grain bread

Remove 12 pieces from the jar of herring tidbits and let them drain. Use the remaining herring tidbits for other purposes. Put the drained pieces in the center of a serving platter. Butter the bread well and cut the slices into 6 pieces. Arrange the buttered bread around the herring pieces and let guests help themselves.

DELICATESSEN TRAY

1 slice of ham or bologna, roast beef, or turkey roll, cut about ½ inch thick
2 slices of liverwurst, cut ½ inch thick

1 gherkin
A few olives (black or green)
Prepared mustard
Ketchup or chili sauce

Have 1 thick slice of whatever you choose, and which does not conflict with your main meat selection, sliced at your delicatessen. Dice the meat, slice the gherkin, and drain the olives. In the center of a serving platter, put a shot glass or egg cup filled with toothpicks. Place a small bowl filled with prepared mustard on one side and one filled with ketchup or chili sauce on the other side. Arrange the diced meats, sliced gherkin, and olives around the dishes and let the guests help themselves.

NUTTY LIVER SPREAD

8 ounces soft liverwurst or canned paté, or chicken liver spread
3–4 tablespoons grated nuts
¼ teaspoon dry mustard

Put liverwurst into a bowl. Mix nuts and dry mustard. Blend nuts into the soft liverwurst and shape the mixture into a ball. If desired, roll the ball in more grated nuts. Refrigerate before serving. Serve with bread or crackers.

SMOKED OYSTERS

One 3½-ounce can smoked oysters
Lemon juice

Drain oysters well, patting them with a paper towel to remove excess oil. Sprinkle with lemon juice and toss. Arrange on a plate surrounded with crackers. A pickle fork is helpful.

LIVERWURST AND ONIONS

3–4 slices of firm liverwurst
About 12 slivers of onion

Cut the slices of liverwurst in half or quarters and arrange on a platter in a ring, leaving the center open. Peel an onion and with a potato peeler cut about 12 thin slivers to arrange in the center of the liverwurst. Serve with a small fork, and, if desired, with crackers on the side.

SHRIMP SPREAD

One 4½-ounce can tiny shrimp
1 tablespoon Durkee Famous Sauce
Lemon juice to taste

Drain shrimp and rinse or not as directed on the can. Put the shrimp
into a bowl, mix with the sauce, and season to taste with lemon juice.
Put the spread into a bowl, arrange it on a plate surrounded with
crackers, and serve with a small spoon.

CRABMEAT SPREAD

One 7½-ounce can crabmeat   *1 teaspoon chopped fresh dill*
A few drops lemon juice   *Salt and pepper to taste*
Mayonnaise

Drain the crabmeat and empty into a bowl. Sprinkle with a few drops
of lemon juice, add just enough mayonnaise to bind, then add chopped
dill. Taste for seasoning, and add more lemon juice if needed. Serve
on crackers.

SARDINE SPREAD

One 3¾-ounce can skinless and boneless sardines
1 teaspoon prepared mustard
Juice of ½ lemon

Empty sardines with oil onto a plate and add mustard and lemon
juice. Mash together with a fork and arrange in a heap in the center
of a platter. Serve surrounded with crackers.

CLAM SPREAD

One 7½-ounce can chopped clams   *1 tablespoon grated onion*
1 teaspoon lemon juice   *2 teaspoons chopped fresh dill*
¾ cup creamed cottage cheese   *Salt and pepper to taste*

Drain clams and shake well. Put them into a bowl, sprinkle with lemon juice, and add the cottage cheese, grated onion, and chopped dill. Mix well and taste for seasoning. Serve with crackers. A small spoon is helpful.

SOUPS

A QUICK VEGETABLE SOUP

1 can onion soup
1 soup can water
One 8½-ounce can Veg-all
Parmesan cheese

Combine the onion soup and water; drain the Veg-all and add it to the soup. Heat to the boiling point. Serve sprinkled with Parmesan cheese.

SERVINGS FOR 4 ARE SMALL.

GREEN PEA AND TOMATO SOUP

1 can green pea soup
1 can tomato bisque
1½ soup cans water
4 cherry tomatoes, sliced

Combine pea soup, tomato bisque, and water. Stir well to blend and heat to the boiling point. Ladle into soup bowls and serve with sliced cherry tomatoes on top.

SERVINGS FOR 4 ARE LARGE.

NUTTY CREAM OF CELERY SOUP

1 can cream of celery soup
1 soup can milk
½ soup can Half & Half
2 tablespoons smooth peanut butter

Combine celery soup with milk and Half & Half, and stir well. Blend the peanut butter into the soup by stirring constantly over a low flame. If desired, serve with grated peanuts on top.

SERVINGS FOR 4 ARE SMALL.

FISH CHOWDER

1 can New England-style clam chowder
1 soup can water
One 8-ounce bottle clam juice
½ pound filet of flounder
½ teaspoon dried thyme

In a saucepan, combine the clam chowder with the water and clam juice. Cut the filet of flounder into bite-sized pieces, add them to the clam chowder along with the thyme, and simmer for 10 minutes.

SERVINGS FOR 4 ARE SMALL.

BLACK BEAN SOUP

This is about the most popular and "elegant" of the canned soups.

One 11-ounce can black bean soup
1 soup can water
¼ cup sherry

GARNISHINGS:
Sliced lemons, or chopped eggs, or chopped onions, or a mixture of chopped eggs and onions.

Blend together the soup, water, and sherry and simmer for 5–10 minutes. Serve with more sherry on the side to float on top. Garnish with sliced lemon, chopped eggs or onions, or a combination of onions and eggs.

SERVINGS FOR 4 ARE SMALL.

A LIGHT POTATO SOUP

One 10¾-ounce can chicken broth
½ soup can water
½ can Half & Half
4 scallions, trimmed, white and
green parts

¾ cup instant potato flakes
½ boneless chicken breast,
uncooked

Combine chicken broth, water, and Half & Half and bring to a simmer. Trim the scallions and snip both the white and green parts into rings with scissors. Add them to the liquid. While stirring constantly, add the potato flakes. Keep the soup at a simmer and gradually it will thicken. Dice the chicken breast, add to the soup, and simmer for 2 minutes.

SERVINGS FOR 4 ARE SMALL.

PART ONE

FISH

FILET OF COD WITH ONIONS

1½–2 pounds cod filet
½ stick margarine (2 ounces)
1 cup frozen chopped onion
½ teaspoon paprika

Preheat oven to 400° F.

Rinse the filet of cod, pat dry, and cut into 4 portions. Arrange the portions, without crowding, in a baking dish. In a separate pan, melt the margarine, add the frozen onions and paprika, and sauté over high heat for a few minutes, until the onions have lost some of their water. Spread the onions evenly over the fish filet. When ready to serve, bake quickly for 15–20 minutes in the preheated oven.

A FISH PIE

Pam
8 small filets of flounder,
       1–1½ pounds in all
Juice of 1 lemon
One 4-ounce can shrimp
4 eggs

1 cup light cream
½ teaspoon pepper
1 bunch scallions, trimmed,
       white and green parts
2 tablespoons grated onion

Preheat oven to 300–325° F.

Spray a 10-inch pie pan with Pam. Put the filets of flounder into a small bowl and sprinkle them with lemon juice. Let stand for 10 minutes, then remove the filets from the juice and pat dry. Cut the fish into bite-sized pieces and arrange them in the pie pan. Open the can of shrimp and rinse or not, according to the directions on can. Add shrimp to the fish in the pie pan. In a bowl, combine eggs, cream, and pepper and beat lightly. Trim the scallions and, with scissors, cut little rings from both the white and green parts into the egg mixture. Add the grated onion and, if desired, some salt, depending on the shrimp used. Pour the egg mixture over the fish and shrimp in the pie pan and bake in the preheated oven for 30–45 minutes, or until the center is set and a knife inserted comes out clean. Be careful to keep the oven temperature at 325° F. tops, or the custard may be watery.

FILET OF COD WITH CAPERS

2–2½ pounds filet of cod
Juice of 1 lemon
3 tablespoons capers

4 tablespoons mayonnaise
2 teaspoons prepared mustard

Preheat oven to 400° F.

Cut the filet of cod into 4 portions. Put them into a bowl and pour lemon juice over them. After 10 minutes remove the fish filets, pat them dry, and arrange in a baking dish that holds them all in a single layer. Combine capers, mayonnaise, and mustard and spread the mixture over the fish filets. When ready to serve, bake in the preheated oven for 15–20 minutes.

BAKED FILET OF COD

2 small filets of cod or scrod, 1½–2 pounds in all
Juice of 1 lemon
About 6 tablespoons bread crumbs
One 14-ounce can marinara sauce

Preheat oven to 400° F.

Rinse fish, pat dry, and arrange in a baking dish large enough to hold the filets in 1 piece. Sprinkle with lemon juice and turn once. After 10 minutes, drain off any liquid and pat dry. Arrange 1 filet at the bottom of the baking dish, sprinkle with half the bread crumbs, and pour on half the marinara sauce. Top with the second filet, sprinkle with bread crumbs, and pour remaining sauce over it. When ready to serve, bake for 20 minutes in the preheated oven. Serve directly from the baking dish.

FILET OF FLOUNDER ROLLS

8 small filets of flounder
Juice of 1 lemon
One 4½-ounce can small shrimp

2 tablespoons Durkee Famous
Sauce
½ cup white wine

Preheat oven to 400° F.

Rinse filets and pat dry. Sprinkle them with lemon juice and let stand for a few minutes. Open and drain canned shrimp. Rinse or not, according to directions on can. Mash shrimp together with the Durkee Famous Sauce; remove fish filets from the lemon juice and pat dry. Spread the shrimp mixture on the fish filets and roll the filets. Put the rolls into a baking dish with the open end at the bottom. When ready to serve, pour wine over the fish rolls, cover with aluminum foil, and bake in the preheated oven for 10 minutes. Serve directly from the baking dish.

FILET OF MACKEREL IN MARINARA SAUCE

2–2½ pounds filet of mackerel
Juice of 2 lemons
One 14-ounce can marinara sauce
Grated Parmesan cheese

Preheat oven to 400° F.

Divide fish filets into 4 portions, rinse them, and pat dry. Sprinkle with lemon juice and let stand for a few minutes. Remove the filets from the juice, pat dry again, and arrange in a single layer in a buttered baking dish. Heat the marinara sauce, sprinkle fish with Parmesan cheese, pour sauce over the fish, and sprinkle with more cheese. When ready to serve, bake in the preheated oven for 10–15 minutes. Serve directly from the baking dish.

BAKED SALMON STEAK

4 salmon steaks, each about 1 inch thick, approximately 2 pounds in all
1 cup white wine
½ cup water

1 bay leaf
½ small onion
Salt and pepper to taste
1 tablespoon cornstarch

Preheat oven to 400° F.

Rinse steaks, pat dry, and arrange in a buttered baking dish in a single layer. In a saucepan, combine wine, water, bay leaf, and onion and simmer for 10 minutes. With a slotted spoon, remove the bay leaf and onion and add salt and pepper. Mix cornstarch with a bit of water and add to the liquid. Simmer for a few seconds to dissolve the cornstarch, and pour over fish. When ready to serve, bake for 10–12 minutes in the preheated oven.

BAKED COD STEAKS WITH MUSTARD SAUCE

4 cod steaks, each about 1 inch thick
Juice of 1 lemon
4 tablespoons butter
1½ tablespoons prepared mustard

Preheat oven to 400° F.

Rinse fish, pat dry, and sprinkle with lemon juice. Let stand. Melt the butter and blend in mustard. Pat fish dry and arrange in a pan large enough to hold fish in a single layer. Spoon melted butter over fish. When ready to serve, bake for 10–15 minutes in the preheated oven.

BAKED FILET OF SOLE

8 small filets of sole, approximately 1½–2 pounds in all
Juice of 3 lemons
4 tablespoons butter
Salt and pepper to taste

Preheat oven to 400° F.

Rinse filets and pat them dry. Fold them over and set in a single layer in a buttered baking dish. In a small saucepan, combine the lemon juice and butter; add salt and pepper and heat until butter is melted. Spoon mixture over folded fish and cover well. When ready to serve, remove cover and bake for 10 minutes in the preheated oven. Serve directly from the baking dish, but be careful because the fish is very fragile.

FISH MEDLEY

1 pound filet of flounder   *3 tablespoons butter*
Juice of ½ lemon   *3 tablespoons flour*
½ pound scallops   *½ cup Half & Half*
1 cup white wine   *½ cup grated American cheese*
One 4½-ounce can shrimp   *Salt and pepper to taste*

Preheat oven to 375° F.

Rinse filets of flounder, pat them dry, and sprinkle with lemon juice. Let stand. Rinse scallops, pick them over for shells and sand, and cut large ones in half. Put the scallops into a saucepan, add wine, and heat to the boiling point. Simmer for 1 minute. Remove scallops from wine with a slotted spoon and put them into a 1-quart baking dish. Remove fish from lemon juice and pat dry. Cut into bite-sized pieces and add to scallops. Open can of shrimp and rinse or not, according to directions on can. Add shrimp to fish and scallops. Melt the butter and blend in the flour. Add the wine in which the scallops have been cooked and blend. Add Half & Half and blend again. Finally, add cheese and simmer until cheese is melted. Season to taste with salt and pepper and pour over fish medley. When ready to serve, bake for 10–15 minutes in the preheated oven.

PAPRIKA FISH

4 haddock steaks (or use cod),	*5 tablespoons butter*
each about 1 inch thick,	*½ cup light cream*
approximately 2 pounds	*1 teaspoon salt*
in all	*½ teaspoon pepper*
1½ cups frozen chopped onion	*1 tablespoon paprika*

Preheat oven to 400° F.

Rinse fish and pat dry. Select a baking dish that holds fish in a single layer. In a saucepan, combine onions and butter and sauté until the onions begin to soften. Spread onions over the bottom of the baking dish and arrange fish on top. To the cream add salt, pepper, and paprika. Heat this mixture to the boiling point and pour it over the fish. When ready to serve, bake for 15 minutes in the preheated oven. Serve directly from the baking dish.

BAKED HALIBUT STEAK

4 halibut steaks, each 1 inch thick,	*5 tablespoons butter*
approximately 2 pounds	*4 tablespoons drained prepared*
in all	*white horseradish*
Juice of 1 lemon	*Salt and pepper to taste*

Preheat oven to 400° F.

Rinse halibut steaks, pat dry, and sprinkle with lemon juice. Let stand for a few minutes, then pat dry again and arrange in a single layer in a buttered baking dish. Melt the butter, blend in drained horseradish, add salt and pepper, and spoon mixture over fish. When ready to serve, bake for 10–15 minutes in the preheated oven. Serve directly from the baking dish.

BAKED SWORDFISH WITH ANCHOVIES

4 portions of swordfish steaks, *¾ stick butter (3 ounces)*
each about 1 inch thick, *6 flat anchovy fillets*
2 pounds in all *4 slices of lemon*
Juice of 1 lemon

Preheat oven to 400° F.

Rinse fish and pat dry. Sprinkle with lemon juice and let stand for a few minutes. Melt butter, add anchovy fillets, and mash them with a fork until smooth. Remove fish from lemon juice, pat dry again, and spread anchovy butter over the steaks. Arrange the fish in a baking dish large enough to hold it in a single layer. Top each steak with a slice of lemon. When ready to serve, bake for 10–15 minutes in the preheated oven. Serve directly from the baking dish.

BAKED FILET OF FLOUNDER IN CLAM JUICE

4 portions of thick filet of *Boiling water*
flounder, approximately *2 tablespoons butter*
1½–2 pounds in all *2 tablespoons flour*
Juice of 2 lemons *Pepper*
One 8-ounce bottle clam juice

Preheat oven to 400° F.

Arrange fish pieces in a baking dish large enough to hold them in a single layer. Combine lemon juice and clam juice, bring to the boiling point, and pour over fish. If the dish is too large, it may be necessary to add enough boiling water just to cover fish. Cover the baking dish with aluminum foil. When ready to serve, bake for 10 minutes in the preheated oven. While fish is baking, blend together butter and flour. When fish is done, pour 1 cup of the baking liquid over the blended butter/flour mixture and stir until smooth. Simmer for a few minutes. Serve fish directly from the baking dish, with sauce on the side.

BAKED FILET OF BLUE FISH

4 small filets of blue fish, approximately 1 1/2–2 pounds in all, or 2 large filets cut into 4 portions
3 tablespoons butter

1 cup frozen chopped onion
1/2 cup frozen chopped green peppers
One 8-ounce can tomato sauce
Salt and pepper to taste

Preheat oven to 400° F.

Rinse filets and pat them dry. Arrange the filets in a buttered baking dish large enough to hold the fish in a single layer. Cover with plastic wrap until the sauce is ready. Melt butter, add onions and green peppers, and sauté for a few minutes. Add tomato sauce and bring to the boiling point. Put the mixture into the top of a double boiler and let ripen until ready to serve. Season with salt and pepper to taste. Remove plastic wrap and pour sauce over fish. Bake for 15 minutes in the preheated oven. Serve directly from the baking dish.

COD STEAKS AND SAUERKRAUT

4 cod steaks, each about 1 inch thick

Juice of 1 lemon

One 16-ounce can sauerkraut

6 tablespoons butter or margarine

1 teaspoon caraway seeds

Preheat oven to 400° F.

Rinse cod steaks and pat dry; sprinkle with lemon juice and let stand. Drain sauerkraut in a colander and press dry; rinse very well and press dry again. In a saucepan, melt butter and add sauerkraut and caraway seeds. Toss until sauerkraut is well coated with fat. Arrange fish steaks in a baking dish in a single layer. Spoon the sauerkraut over the fish, piling it high. When ready to serve, bake for 15 minutes in the preheated oven.

MEAT AND POULTRY

BREAST OF CHICKEN WITH HORSERADISH SAUCE

4 whole boneless chicken breasts, cut in half (8 pieces in all)
Pam
One 10½-ounce can chicken gravy
One 4-ounce jar red horseradish, drained and pressed dry

Preheat oven to 400° F.

Trim off fat from chicken pieces. Select a baking dish large enough to hold all the chicken in a single layer. Spray with Pam and arrange chicken pieces in the dish. Put chicken gravy into a saucepan. Drain horseradish, press dry, and add it to the gravy. Bring the mixture to the boiling point and pour over the chicken pieces. When ready to serve, bake in the preheated oven for 15–20 minutes.

CHICKEN CHINESE

3 whole boneless chicken breasts, cut in half (6 pieces in all)
Two 10-ounce packages frozen Chinese vegetables
2–3 cups cooked rice
Soy sauce

Trim chicken breasts and cut into bite-sized pieces. Add water to the vegetables according to package instructions, and bring to the boiling point. Simmer for 1 minute, then add the cut-up chicken. Continue cooking until vegetables are done, but still crisp. Serve over cooked rice with soy sauce on the side.

BREAST OF CHICKEN AND CLAM SAUCE

4 whole boneless chicken breasts, cut in half (8 pieces in all)
2 teaspoons dried thyme
Pam
Two 8-ounce cans white clam sauce

Preheat oven to 400° F.

Trim chicken breasts of fat. Arrange the chicken on waxed paper, sprinkle with thyme, cover with another piece of waxed paper, and pound lightly to press herb into meat. Remove the waxed paper from the chicken breasts, turn the chicken pieces, sprinkle again with thyme, cover, and pound lightly. Select a baking dish large enough to hold the chicken pieces in a single layer. Spray it with Pam and add the chicken pieces. In another pan bring the white clam sauce to the boiling point, then pour it over the chicken. When ready to serve, bake for 15–20 minutes in the preheated oven.

BREAST OF CHICKEN WITH
TOMATO SAUCE AND CHEESE

This is, of course, a variation of *veal parmigiana*. The chicken, however, is neither breaded nor fried.

4 whole boneless chicken breasts, cut in half (8 pieces in all)
2 teaspoons dried basil
2–3 tablespoons grated Parmesan cheese

Pam
Two 8-ounce cans your favorite spaghetti sauce
4 square slices of Muenster cheese, cut in half

Preheat oven to 400° F.

Trim chicken breasts of fat, arrange on waxed paper, sprinkle with basil and Parmesan cheese, cover with another piece of waxed paper, and pound lightly. Remove waxed paper, turn chicken pieces, sprinkle with basil and cheese, and lightly pound again. Select a pan large enough to hold the chicken pieces in a single layer. Spray with Pam and arrange chicken pieces in the pan. In a saucepan, heat the spaghetti sauce, pour it over the chicken, and top each piece with ½ slice of Muenster cheese. Then sprinkle the whole with Parmesan cheese. When ready to serve, bake for 15–20 minutes in the preheated oven.

BAKED CHICKEN LEGS

Pam
8 chicken legs
Paprika

Margarine
½ cup hot water

Preheat oven to 375° F.

Spray a rimmed cookie sheet with Pam. Look chicken legs over carefully. If they have fat layers under the skin, just sprinkle heavily with paprika and arrange on the cookie sheet in a single layer. If they are lean, melt about 3 tablespoons margarine, blend in 1 tablespoon paprika, and brush chicken legs with the mixture. Bake for 30 minutes in the preheated oven, then add ½ cup hot water and continue baking for another 15–20 minutes.

BREAST OF CHICKEN IN TARRAGON SAUCE

4 whole boneless chicken breasts, cut in half (8 pieces in all)
Pam
1 cup white wine
½ teaspoon dried tarragon
6 tablespoons butter
6 tablespoons flour
2 cups Half & Half

Preheat oven to 400° F.

Trim chicken breasts of fat, and select a baking dish large enough to hold them in a single layer. Spray with Pam and arrange chicken pieces in the dish. To 1 cup of white wine, add tarragon and simmer. Melt the butter, add flour and blend; then add Half & Half and stir until smooth. Add the wine and tarragon to the cream sauce and pour over chicken pieces. When ready to serve, bake in the preheated oven for 15–20 minutes.

BREAST OF CHICKEN WITH MUSHROOMS

4 whole boneless chicken breasts,
cut in half (8 pieces in
all)
Pam
One 8-ounce can mushrooms,
pieces and stems

6 tablespoons butter
6 tablespoons flour
2½ cups Half & Half
½ cup dry vermouth
Salt and pepper to taste

Preheat oven to 400° F.

Select a baking dish large enough to hold the chicken pieces in a
single layer. Spray with Pam and arrange chicken breasts in the pan.
Drain mushrooms and sprinkle them over the breasts. Melt butter, add
flour and blend. Add Half & Half and stir well until smooth. Add
vermouth and season with salt and pepper to taste. Simmer for a few
minutes, then pour over the chicken breasts. When ready to serve, bake
for 15–20 minutes in the preheated oven.

HAM AND RED CABBAGE

One 16-ounce jar red cabbage
1½ pounds ham steak, ready to
eat, cut into 4 portions,
or use 4 slices of canned
ham

Pam
¾ cup red wine

Preheat oven to 325° F.

Drain cabbage in a colander and press dry. Select a baking dish large
enough to hold the ham portions in a single layer; spray with Pam.
Put drained cabbage into pan, top with the 4 portions of ham, and
pour the red wine over the whole. Cover with aluminum foil and bake

for 30–40 minutes in the preheated oven. Serve directly from the baking dish.

MOCK HAM AND CHICKEN POT PIE

Approximately 1 pound ready-to-eat or canned ham
2 whole boneless chicken breasts, cut in half (4 pieces in all)

One 10½-ounce can chicken gravy
½ cup sherry
One 8-ounce can mushrooms, pieces and stems
1 package frozen crescent rolls

Preheat oven to 375° F.

Dice the ham and uncooked chicken, and combine with chicken gravy and sherry. Drain mushrooms and add. Put the mixture into a 1½–2-quart baking dish. A half-hour before serving, place in the preheated oven. Take crescent rolls apart, but do not roll; arrange the 8 triangles on a cookie sheet and bake in a 375° F. oven for 15–20 minutes. To serve, put 1 triangle at the bottom, cover with the ham/chicken mixture, and top with the second triangle.

HAM AND FRUITS

1½–2 pounds ready-to-eat ham steak, or use slices of canned ham, or slices of ready-to-eat smoked pork loin, also called Canadian bacon
Two 10-ounce cans mandarin oranges
¼ cup orange juice

Preheat oven to 350° F.

Cut ham slices into 4 portions. Select a baking dish large enough to hold ham pieces in a single overlapping layer. Rinse ham pieces and pat dry. Drain mandarin oranges and reserve juice. Arrange some fruit sections in the bottom of the dish and place ham pieces overlapping on top. Scatter remaining fruit over ham and add the reserved liquid and orange juice. Cover with aluminum foil and bake in the preheated oven for 30 minutes. Serve directly from the baking dish.

VARIATIONS:

Instead of mandarin oranges, use unsweetened pineapple chunks and pineapple juice.

Use cranberry-orange relish and cranberry juice.

Use grapes, fresh or canned, and white wine.

Use fresh apple slices and apple juice.

SAUERKRAUT AND GARNISHINGS

This is an adaptation of the classic Alsatian *choucroute garni.*

2 pounds sauerkraut	*use 4 portions of ready-to-*
1½–2 quarts apple juice	*eat ham steaks*
4 ready-to-eat Canadian-type	*4 knackwursts*
boneless pork chops, or	*4 frankfurters*

Drain sauerkraut in a large colander and rinse very well with water; press dry. Put it into a 2–2½-quart casserole with a lid and add enough apple juice to cover. Bring to the boiling point, then reduce heat and simmer. The longer the sauerkraut cooks the better it will be, so put it on first thing. Add more juice as needed. About 20 minutes before serving, place the pork chops or ham portions on top of the sauerkraut and cover. Put knackwursts and frankfurters into a large pot with water and bring to the boiling point. Do not boil because the skins may burst, and do not cover. Just let them stand in the hot water. When ready to serve, remove pork from sauerkraut and keep warm. Drain the sauerkraut, but reserve the liquid in case there are leftovers to be reheated. Arrange sauerkraut on an oval platter, heaping it high, with the pork chops on top, and surround with sausages. Serve with parsley potatoes and mustard on the side.

HAM IN MADEIRA

1½–2 pounds ready-to-eat ham
½ cup raisins
2 cups Madeira
1 tablespoon cornstarch

Preheat oven to 375° F.

Cut ham into 4 portions or leave in 1 or 2 slices, but be sure to trim off rind so the ham will not curl. Select a baking dish that will hold the ham in a single layer. Sprinkle the bottom with raisins, arrange ham on top, pour the Maderia over the whole, and cover with aluminum foil. When ready to serve, bake for 20 minutes in the preheated oven. Remove ham and keep warm. Pour wine and raisins into a saucepan, and moisten cornstarch with some water. Bring the wine mixture to the boiling point, and slowly, while stirring constantly, add enough cornstarch to thicken sauce to desired consistency. This will depend upon how much wine has evaporated during baking. Serve with sauce on the side.

HAM IN RED WINE AND ONIONS

1½–2 pounds ready-to-eat ham
One 16-ounce can white onions
½ cup beef gravy
½ cup red wine

Preheat oven to 400° F.

Trim ham slices and cut into 4 portions. Arrange ham in a single overlapping layer in a baking dish. Drain onions in a colander and rinse with hot water. Shake dry and arrange around ham pieces. Combine beef gravy and wine, and bring to the boiling point. Pour over ham and onions, and cover the dish with aluminum foil. When ready to serve, bake for 15–20 minutes in the preheated oven.

HAM AND APPLE HORSERADISH SAUCE

4 portions of ready-to-eat ham steaks, approximately 2 pounds in all
2 cups applesauce
One 4-ounce jar prepared white horseradish, drained and pressed dry

Preheat oven to 375° F.

Trim ham pieces and wipe with a damp towel. Arrange in a single overlapping layer in a buttered baking dish. Put applesauce into a saucepan. Drain horseradish in a colander and press dry. Add the horseradish to the applesauce, mix, and heat to just below the boiling point. Spread over ham slices. When ready to serve, bake for 20 minutes in the preheated oven.

MINIATURE MEAT LOAVES

1 egg	*½ teaspoon dried marjoram*
2 tablespoons ketchup	*½ teaspoon pepper*
⅓ cup dry bread crumbs	*1½ pounds ground beef*
2 teaspoons soy sauce	*4 tablespoons frozen chopped onion*
½ teaspoon dried thyme	*One 8-ounce can tomato sauce*

Preheat oven to 375° F.

In a bowl, combine egg, ketchup, bread crumbs, soy sauce, thyme, marjoram, and pepper; mix well, add the beef, and blend. Divide into 4 portions. Take 1 tablespoon of the frozen onions and shape 1 portion of the beef mixture around the onions so the onions are in the center. Shape into balls, then drop them onto the table, and flatten the top. Arrange on a baking sheet. When ready to serve, bake for 20 minutes in the preheated oven. Bring the tomato sauce to the boiling point and serve on the side.

BEEF PIZZA

Pam	*4 slices of white bread, toasted*
1–1¼ pounds ground beef (ground	*1 cup shredded Cheddar cheese*
sirloin preferred)	*1 cup tomato sauce*

Preheat oven to 400° F.

Select a baking dish large enough to hold the 4 slices of bread in a single layer, and spray with Pam. Divide the meat into 4 portions, shaping them very lightly into 4 patties. Put the toast into the baking dish and place the patties on top of the bread slices, being careful not to press them together. Combine cheese and tomato sauce, and spoon over the patties, dividing the mixture evenly and piling it high. Bake for 20 minutes in the preheated oven until the cheese bubbles.

NUTTY BEEF BALLS

1½ pounds ground beef
4 tablespoons chopped parsley
2 tablespoons grated onion
1 teaspoon salt

¾ cup almond slivers (about
2½ ounces)
Two 8-ounce cans tomato
sauce

Preheat oven to 400° F.

Combine beef, parsley, onion, salt, and almond slivers. Divide into 4 equal portions, shape into balls about 1 inch thick, and set in a baking dish. Then pour tomato sauce over the beef patties. When ready to serve, bake in the preheated oven for 25–30 minutes. Serve directly from the baking dish.

VEAL AND PIMENTOS

1½ pounds ground veal
4 tablespoons chopped pimentos
1 teaspoon salt
½ teaspoon pepper

One 10¾-ounce can cream of
mushroom soup
One 4-ounce can button
mushrooms

Preheat oven to 400° F.

Combine meat, chopped pimentos, salt, and pepper and shape into 4 patties, each about ½ inch thick. Combine mushroom soup with mushrooms and their liquid, and bring to the boiling point. Pour over patties. When ready to serve, bake for 20–25 minutes in the preheated oven.

VEAL PATTIES AND CAPERS

1½ pounds ground veal   *Juice of 1 lemon*
3 tablespoons capers, drained   *2–3 tablespoons sour cream*
½ teaspoon pepper

Preheat oven to 400° F.

Mix veal, capers, pepper, and lemon juice and shape into 8 patties, each about ½ inch thick. When ready to serve, bake in the preheated oven for 20–25 minutes. Remove patties and keep warm. To the pan juices add the sour cream and blend well. Reheat just to the boiling point (do not boil because the cream will curdle) and pour over the patties.

VEAL STEW AND RED WINE

2 pounds stewing veal   *Red wine to cover*
1 cup frozen chopped onion   *Salt and pepper to taste*
1 bay leaf   *2 tablespoons cornstarch*

Preheat oven to 375° F.

In a flameproof casserole, combine veal, onion, bay leaf, and add enough wine to cover. Simmer on top of the stove for 10–15 minutes, then cover and bake for 30–40 minutes in the preheated oven, until the meat is fork tender. (If no flameproof casserole is available, cook stew first in a pot, then transfer it to a baking dish and cover with aluminum foil before baking.) Drain off liquid. Mix cornstarch with a bit of water to moisten. Bring cooking liquid to the boiling point and add some of the cornstarch. Simmer until desired thickness is reached. Add to meat, reheat, and serve.

VEAL CHOPS WITH GREEN SAUCE

4 rib veal chops, each about   *4 thick scallions, both white and*
½ inch thick   *green parts, trimmed and*
One 10½-ounce can chicken   *snipped into rings*
gravy   *⅛ teaspoon dried tarragon*
2 tablespoons chopped parsley   *½ cup dry vermouth*

Preheat oven to 400° F.

Rinse chops and pat them dry; arrange in a baking dish large enough to hold them in a single layer. In a saucepan, combine chicken gravy with parsley, scallion rings, and tarragon; add vermouth and beat until smooth. Bring to the boiling point and simmer for 2–3 minutes. Pour over chops. When ready to serve, bake in the preheated oven for 30–35 minutes.

N O T E :
Thinner chops will bake faster while thicker chops may take a bit longer.

LAMB PATTIES IN A CURRY SAUCE WITH BANANAS

1½ pounds ground lamb   *One 10½-ounce can chicken*
½ teaspoon salt   *gravy*
1 tablespoon grated onion   *1 tablespoon curry powder*
3 bananas   *2 tablespoons peanut butter*

Preheat oven to 400° F.

Season lamb with salt, add grated onion and blend. Divide into 8 small patties and put into a baking dish large enough to hold them without crowding. Peel and slice the bananas about ½ inch thick and scatter over and around the lamb patties. Combine chicken gravy, curry powder, and peanut butter in a saucepan and, stirring constantly, gently heat the gravy while blending in the peanut butter. Pour over lamb patties and bananas. When ready to serve, bake in the preheated oven for 20 minutes.

LAMB STEAKS OR LAMB SHOULDER CHOPS
WITH ONIONS

4 lamb steaks or shoulder chops, each ½ inch thick	3 tablespoons flour
2 tablespoons butter	1½ cups Half & Half
2 cups frozen chopped onion	1 teaspoon salt
1 teaspoon paprika	½ teaspoon pepper

Preheat oven to 400° F.

Rinse steaks or chops and pat dry. Melt butter and quickly sear meat on both sides, then arrange in a baking dish large enough to hold steaks or chops in a single layer. To the fat in the pan add onions and sauté for a minute, then add paprika and dust with flour; add Half & Half, salt, and pepper. Cook until sauce is thickened. Spread over meat pieces. When ready to serve, bake in the preheated oven for 15 minutes.

VEGETABLES

BAKED BROCCOLI

One 10-ounce package frozen chopped broccoli
One 10½-ounce can cream of asparagus soup
¼ teaspoon nutmeg
1–2 tablespoons grated cheese

Cook broccoli according to package instructions, but keep it under-done. Drain broccoli and put it into a baking dish along with the soup and nutmeg. Sprinkle with cheese. When ready to serve, bake for 15–20 minutes at 350–400° F., with whatever else is in the oven.

CAULIFLOWER AND CHERRY TOMATOES

One 10½-ounce package frozen cauliflower
¼ teaspoon nutmeg
6 cherry tomatoes

Cook cauliflower according to package instructions, but add the nutmeg. Quarter the tomatoes. When cauliflower is done, drain well, return to saucepan, add quartered tomatoes, and reheat briefly, shaking the pan constantly to prevent sticking.

SWEET POTATO CASSEROLE

One 16-ounce can sweet potatoes or yams
2 tablespoons brown sugar
2 tablespoons butter
1 lemon

Preheat oven to 375° F.

Arrange the sweet potatoes in a pie pan or other baking dish; pour liquid from can over potatoes, sprinkle with brown sugar, and dot with butter. Trim lemon on both ends and then slice thin. Arrange lemon slices on top of potatoes and bake for 20–25 minutes in the preheated oven. If you are already using the oven on a higher temperature, put the potatoes in with whatever is cooking and reduce the baking time accordingly.

INSTANT MASHED POTATOES

Approximately 1½ cups dry instant potato flakes
4–5 tablespoons sour cream

Prepare potatoes according to package instructions, then add the sour cream instead of butter and milk.

VARIATIONS:

1) Add 2 tablespoons fresh scallions cut into rings.
2) Add 1 tablespoon grated onion.
3) Add buttermilk instead of milk.
4) Add 3 tablespoons grated American cheese and reheat until cheese is melted, or put into a baking dish and bake for 10 minutes with whatever is in the oven.

GREEN BEANS AND TOMATO SAUCE

One 10½-ounce package frozen French-cut green beans
One 8-ounce can tomato sauce
¼ teaspoon dried basil

Cook beans according to package instructions. Heat tomato sauce and add basil. When beans are done, drain well and add to tomato sauce. Reheat before serving.

SPINACH AND ONIONS

One 10½-ounce package frozen chopped spinach
½ cup frozen chopped onion
½ stick butter (2 ounces)

Cook spinach according to package instructions. Drain very well and return to saucepan. Combine onions and butter in a frying pan and, over low heat, sauté onions until light brown. Add to spinach and blend well.

ASPARAGUS WITH LEMON

1 lemon   _Two 10½-ounce packages frozen_
2 cups water   _asparagus spears_
1 teaspoon salt   _½ stick butter (2 ounces), optional_

Squeeze the lemon, reserve the juice, and put pressed shells into a saucepan with the water and salt. Bring to the boiling point, add asparagus, and cook until just tender. Drain and discard lemon shells. Place asparagus on a serving platter, heat lemon juice to lukewarm and pour over asparagus. Baste several times. If desired, add butter to the lemon juice and use lemon butter for the sauce.

ZUCCHINI

6 medium-sized zucchini
1 teaspoon salt
2 tablespoons butter

Scrub zucchini, trim, and cut into quarters. Place in a saucepan with enough water to cover and add salt. Bring to the boiling point and simmer for 1–2 minutes. Drain, return to pan, and add butter. Shake the pot to distribute butter evenly.

LIMA BEANS AND TOMATOES

One 10½-ounce package frozen lima beans
One 8-ounce can peeled tomatoes

Cook lima beans according to package instructions but keep them underdone. Drain and return to saucepan. Open can of tomatoes and drain over lima beans. Chop the pulp of the tomatoes, add tomato pulp to beans, and reheat the whole.

SALADS

CARROT AND ONION SALAD

*Two 7½-ounce cans carrots, either
    julienned or diced
Juice of 1 lemon
3 scallions, trimmed, white and
    green parts*

*Sour cream
Salt and pepper to taste
4 lettuce leaves*

Drain carrots, put them into a bowl, and sprinkle with lemon juice. Trim scallions and snip both the white and green parts into fine rings. Add to carrots and mix. Gradually add just enough sour cream to bind, and season with salt and pepper. Arrange lettuce leaves on 4 salad plates, and divide the carrot and onion salad among them. Refrigerate before serving.

ORANGE, GRAPEFRUIT, AND ENDIVE SALAD

1 pint fresh grapefruit and orange sections, or
grapefruit sections alone
3 Belgian endives
Mayonnaise
2 tablespoons slivered almonds

Drain citrus sections very well and put them into a bowl. Cut endives into ½–¾-inch pieces, rinse, and pat dry with paper towels or spin dry. Add endive to citrus sections with just enough mayonnaise to bind. Divide among 4 salad plates and sprinkle with slivered almonds.

ARTICHOKE HEARTS

8 Boston lettuce leaves *Mayonnaise*
One 14-ounce jar artichoke hearts *Chopped parsley*
Juice of 1 lemon

Arrange lettuce leaves on 4 salad plates. Drain and rinse artichoke hearts; spin dry or pat with paper towels. Put into a bowl, sprinkle with lemon juice, and refrigerate. Just before serving divide the hearts among the 4 salad plates, put a dab of mayonnaise on top of each portion, and sprinkle with chopped parsley.

FANCY MEDLEY SALAD

4 romaine lettuce leaves *2 bananas*
8 slices of tomato *Lemon French Dressing (see page 45)*
1 avocado

Wash and dry the lettuce and put 1 leaf on each of 4 salad plates. Arrange a slice of tomato at each end of the lettuce leaf. Cut avocado in half and remove the pit, cut each half in half, and dice the meat on the skin. Remove diced avocado meat with a knife or a spoon and place it next to the tomatoes. Peel bananas and cut each in half crosswise. Slice each half into circles and arrange in the center of the lettuce leaf. Carefully spoon dressing over the bananas, avocado, and tomatoes, making sure that each piece is well covered. Refrigerate before serving.

TOMATOES SANDWICH SALAD

8 large slices of tomato
1 pound coleslaw from the delicatessen
4 sprigs watercress

Arrange 4 slices of tomato on 4 salad plates. Put coleslaw into a colander, drain until fairly dry. Divide into 4 servings and pile coleslaw on top of the tomato slice, shaping it like a hamburger. Top each serving with another slice of tomato and stick a sprig of watercress into the middle like a toothpick.

GREEN BEAN AND CUCUMBER SALAD

One 16-ounce can French-cut green beans
1 fresh cucumber
1 tablespoon grated onion

Mayonnaise and Yoghurt dressing (see page 45)
Chopped parsley

Drain beans and put into a bowl. Peel the cucumber and cut it in half lengthwise, removing the seeds and dicing each half. Add to the beans along with the grated onion and just enough dressing to bind. Divide among 4 salad plates and sprinkle each portion with chopped parsley.

MEXICAN SALAD

One 14-ounce can corn niblets	*One 2-ounce can pimentos,*
1 medium-sized tomato	*chopped*
2 tablespoons diced green peppers	*French Dressing (see page 186)*
	or mayonnaise

Drain corn niblets and place in a bowl. Slice the tomato and dice; add to corn along with the diced green peppers and chopped pimentos. Add just enough French dressing to moisten well or just enough mayonnaise to bind. Divide among 4 salad plates and refrigerate before serving.

HEARTS OF PALM AND WATERCRESS SALAD

One 14-ounce can hearts of palm
1 bunch watercress
8 tablespoons French Dressing (see page 186)

Open can of hearts of palm and cut each stalk into ½–¾-inch pieces. Cut hard stems from watercress, wash leaves, and dry. Add to hearts of palm. Add French dressing and toss. All pieces should be well coated with dressing. If not, add more French dressing. Divide among 4 salad plates and refrigerate before serving.

CUCUMBER TOMATO SALAD

1 cucumber
16 cherry tomatoes
4 tablespoons mayonnaise
1 tablespoon plain yoghurt

1 tablespoon chopped fresh dill
Salt and pepper to taste
4 lettuce leaves

Peel cucumber and cut in half crosswise. Cut each half in half again lengthwise, leaving 4 shells, and remove seeds. Rince cherry tomatoes, pat dry, cut into quarters, and put them into a bowl. Combine the mayonnaise, yoghurt, and dill and season with salt and pepper to taste. Add this mixture to the tomato quarters. Put a lettuce leaf on each of 4 salad plates, top with cucumber shells, and fill the shells with the tomatoes. Refrigerate before serving.

BELGIAN ENDIVES, TOMATOES, AND WATERCRESS

16 sprigs watercress
2 Belgian endives
12 cherry tomatoes
French Dressing (see page 186)

Rinse watercress and dry. Trim off hard stems and arrange 4 sprigs on each of 4 salad plates in a star pattern. Cut endives into ¾–1-inch pieces and put them into a bowl. Cut cherry tomatoes in half and add to endives. Add enough French dressing to cover well. Divide among the 4 salad plates on top of the watercress. Spoon an extra teaspoon of dressing over each serving.

LEMON FRENCH DRESSING

½ cup olive or salad oil
3 tablespoons lemon juice
½ teaspoon salt
¼ teaspoon paprika

Whip all the ingredients together in a bowl, refrigerate, then whip again before using.

MAYONNAISE AND YOGHURT DRESSING

½ cup mayonnaise
4 tablespoons plain yoghurt
¼ teaspoon pepper
¼ teaspoon ketchup

Beat all the ingredients together well and refrigerate before serving.

DESSERTS

PEARS WITH ICE CREAM AND CHOCOLATE SAUCE

This is based on the famous pears *Hélène,* named after Jacques Offen-
bach's *La Belle Hélène*

4 large or 8 small canned pear halves   *6 tablespoons chocolate syrup*
½ cup water   *4 scoops vanilla ice cream*
2 teaspoons instant coffee

Arrange either 1 large or 2 small pear halves in each of 4 sherbet
glasses. Chill. Bring water to the boiling point and add instant coffee.
Stir to dissolve, then add chocolate syrup. Keep the sauce hot in a
warm oven. When ready to serve, add a scoop of ice cream to each
glass and divide the sauce among the 4 servings.

PINEAPPLE AND CREME DE CACAO

One 20-ounce can unsweetened pineapple chunks
4 tablespoons crème de cacao

Divide pineapple chunks among 4 dessert dishes; refrigerate as long as possible. Just before serving add 1 tablespoon crème de cacao to each portion.

HASTY FRUIT SALAD

1 pint orange and grapefruit
sections
One 8½-ounce can sliced peaches
One 8½-ounce can pitted black
cherries

Sour cream, optional
Sugar and cinnamon, optional
(4 tablespoons sugar and
1 teaspoon powdered
cinnamon)

Drain orange and grapefruit sections, sliced peaches and cherries, and use juices for other purposes. Combine fruits and divide among 4 dessert dishes. Refrigerate as long as possible. If desired, top each portion with sour cream and sprinkle with sugar and cinnamon.

FANCY APPLESAUCE

2½ cups applesauce
½ cup sour cream
3 tablespoons rum or brandy

2 tablespoons cocoa
2 tablespoons confectioners' sugar

Combine applesauce with sour cream and beat with a wire whisk; add rum or brandy and beat some more. Divide among 4 dessert dishes, and refrigerate as long as possible. Mix cocoa and sugar and sprinkle over applesauce just before serving.

PINK CHERRIES

1–2 cans pitted black cherries (14 ounces in all)
3 tablespoons sour cream
1 tablespoon kirschwasser or rum

Drain cherries, divide among 4 serving glasses, and reserve 1 table-spoon of the juice. Mix sour cream with the reserved cherry juice and 1 tablespoon kirschwasser or rum. Pour the sauce over the cherries and refrigerate before serving.

CHOCOLATE ICE CREAM AND VANILLA SAUCE

1 package instant vanilla pudding   *2 tablespoons grated nuts (pecans,*
1½ cups milk   *walnuts, hazelnuts,*
1 cup light cream   *almonds)*
4 scoops chocolate ice cream

Put the vanilla pudding powder into a saucepan, add the milk and, while stirring constantly, bring to the boiling point. Simmer for 3 seconds, remove from heat, and add light cream; beat together and refrigerate. When ready to serve, put a scoop of ice cream in a dessert dish, add vanilla sauce, and sprinkle with nuts.

VANILLA ICE CREAM WITH PINK SAUCE

8 tablespoons currant jelly
2 tablespoons rum or brandy
4 scoops vanilla ice cream

Put currant jelly into a small saucepan and, while stirring constantly over low heat, liquefy jelly. Just before serving add rum or brandy to liquefied jelly. Put ice cream into sherbet glasses and pour pink sauce over it.

ORANGE SHERBET AND CRUSHED PINEAPPLE

4 scoops orange sherbet
8 teaspoons rum
One 8-ounce can crushed pineapple

Put sherbet into serving dishes. Combine rum and crushed pineapple and spoon over the sherbet.

CAKE AND FRUITS

1 package instant vanilla pudding
2 cups milk
One 16- or 17-ounce can fruit cocktail
4 slices of pound cake

Put vanilla pudding powder into a saucepan, add milk, and, while stirring constantly, bring to the boiling point. Simmer for 3 seconds, then remove from heat. Drain the fruit cocktail, add ¾ cup of the liquid to the vanilla pudding, and refrigerate. When ready to serve, cut cake slices in half, place one half on each of 4 dessert plates, pile fruit cocktail on top, and cover with other half slice of cake. Finally, divide the vanilla sauce among the 4 servings.

FANCY MELON RING

1 small cantaloupe or honeydew melon
4 scoops ice cream
3 tablespoons chopped nuts (any except peanuts)

Cut 4 slices from the middle of the melon, reserving the end pieces for other uses. Discard the seeds and cut off the rind. Refrigerate. When ready to serve, place melon rings on 4 dessert plates and fill centers with 4 scoops of ice cream; then sprinkle with nuts.

A SORT OF TRIFLE

1 package instant lemon pudding
1½ cups milk
½ cup light cream

3 tablespoons rum or other liqueur
8 lady fingers
2 kumquats, cut in half

Put lemon pudding powder into a saucepan and add milk. While stirring constantly, bring to the boiling point and simmer for 5–6 seconds. Remove from heat and stir in light cream and 1 tablespoon of the rum or liqueur; cover top with waxed paper and refrigerate. Cut lady fingers in half and arrange in sherbet glasses, 4 halves to each glass. Moisten lady fingers with the remaining rum or liqueur. When ready to serve, fill glasses with pudding and top with kumquat halves.

FANCY VANILLA PUDDING

1 package instant vanilla pudding
1½ cups milk
½ cup light cream
4 tablespoons apple jelly

1 tablespoon apricot butter or marmalade
4 walnut halves

Put vanilla pudding powder into a saucepan and add milk. While stirring constantly, bring to the boiling point and cook for 10 seconds; remove from heat and stir in cream. Divide among 4 serving glasses and refrigerate. Melt apple jelly and add apricot butter or marmalade. Keep warm. Allow pudding to cool for about 30 minutes, and when a skin has formed on top, gently float the apply jelly apricot sauce on top and garnish with nut halves. Refrigerate again until ready to serve.

CHOCOLATE ICE CREAM WITH CREME DE MENTHE

4 scoops chocolate ice cream
8 teaspoons crème de menthe, white or green

Put ice cream into 4 sherbet glasses and add 2 teaspoons of crème de menthe to each serving.

GRAPES AND VANILLA SAUCE

1 package instant vanilla pudding   *½ cup light cream*
1½ cups milk   *1½–2 cups fresh seedless grapes*
2 tablespoons grape jelly

Put vanilla pudding powder into a saucepan and add the milk and grape jelly. While stirring constantly, bring to the boiling point. Stir until grape jelly has dissolved, then remove from heat and add cream. Rinse the grapes, remove stems, pat them dry with paper towels, and add to the pudding. Cover with waxed paper and refrigerate. When ready to serve, divide among 4 serving dishes.

PART TWO

(ALL THE RECIPES ARE FOR SIX)

PART TWO

HORS D'OEUVRES

CREAM CHEESE AND RADISHES

4 ounces cream cheese, at room temperature
¾ cup grated radishes
1 teaspoon salt

Let cream cheese come to room temperature. Rinse and trim radishes and grate on the coarse side of a household grater. Mix grated radishes with cream cheese and salt. Refrigerate and serve on crackers.

EGGS IN TOMATOES

6 small egg tomatoes   *3 medium or 2 large eggs*
½ teaspoon curry powder   *1 tablespoon butter*
1 tablespoon milk   *12 watercress leaves*
1 teaspoon salt

Wash tomatoes, trim on both ends, and cut through the middle. Scoop out seeds and stand, cut side down, on a paper towel to drain. Blend curry powder, milk, and salt, then add to eggs and beat until well blended. Melt butter, add seasoned eggs, and scramble over low heat. Stand tomato halves up and, if they do not stand straight, trim bottoms a bit more. Spoon scrambled eggs into tomato halves and refrigerate. Just before serving put a watercress leaf into each tomato half.

TUNA EGGS

6 hard-cooked eggs	About ½ cup loosely packed fresh
1 cup Clamato juice	dill leaves
1 envelope plain gelatin	Salt, if desired
One 6- or 7-ounce can tuna fish,	2 tablespoons sherry
drained	Paprika, for garnish

Peel hard-cooked eggs and cut in half crosswise through the middle; reserve egg yolks for other purposes. Trim the egg-white halves at the bottom so they will stand straight. Pour Clamato juice into a small saucepan, sprinkle with gelatin, and heat gently, stirring constantly to dissolve gelatin. Let cool a bit, then add drained tuna. Place mixture into a blender and purée. Gradually add fresh dill leaves and continue to purée until very smooth. Add optional salt and sherry and blend some more. Put into a small bowl and refrigerate. When the mixture begins to jell, stir it up a bit, then spoon into egg-white cups and let set completely. Garnish with a dash of paprika before serving.

SPLIT OLIVES WITH CHICKEN OR TURKEY BREASTS

12 pitted black olives
12 small cubes of cooked chicken or turkey breast
12 toothpicks

Cut the olives in half lengthwise, insert a toothpick, then add a cube of chicken or turkey and the other olive half, so it looks like a whole olive with a meat filling.

SHRIMP ASPIC

One 8-ounce bottle clam juice   *Two 4½-ounce cans of tiny*
½ cup water   *shrimp*
1 envelope plain gelatin   *Juice of 1 lemon*
                               2 teaspoons chopped fresh dill

Pour clam juice into a saucepan, add water, sprinkle with gelatin, and heat until the gelatin dissolves. Add drained shrimp to the clam juice along with lemon juice and chopped dill. Let stand until the mixture begins to thicken, then spoon into a 6-inch aluminum foil cake pan and refrigerate until completely set. Slice and serve with crackers or use as a first course.

TUNA ANCHOVY SPREAD

One 3½-ounce can pitted black olives
4 tablespoons mayonnaise
One 2-ounce can anchovies
One 6- or 7-ounce can tuna fish, drained

Drain olives and put a few at a time into a blender; chop, then empty the blender and add more. When all the olives are chopped, do not clean the blender, but add the mayonnaise first, then the anchovies with their oil, and finally the drained tuna. Purée, remove from blender, and mix with the chopped black olives. Refrigerate and serve with toast or crackers.

LIPTAUER CHEESE

8 ounces cream cheese, at room
    temperature
½ stick butter (2 ounces), at room
    temperature
2 drained anchovy fillets

½ tablespoon grated onion
½ tablespoon caraway seed
Salt to taste
1 tablespoon drained capers
2 teaspoons paprika

Bring cream cheese and butter to room temperature and place in a bowl. Mash anchovies with a fork or chop very fine and add to cream cheese along with the grated onion. Crush the caraway seeds and add; taste for salt, then add drained capers and paprika. Work everything together and shape into a roll. Wrap in waxed paper and refrigerate overnight. Serve with pumpernickel bread and radishes and olives on the side.

WATER CHESTNUTS AND ANCHOVIES

6 water chestnuts
4 anchovy fillets
Toothpicks

Drain and dry water chestnuts, then cut each one in half. Drain anchovy fillets and pat dry. Cut each fillet into 3 equal pieces. Put a piece of anchovy on half a water chestnut and secure with a toothpick. Refrigerate overnight.

HAM AND PICKLE ROLLS

4 slices of ham
1 pickle
12 toothpicks
Chopped parsley or paprika

Select 4 slices of ham the size and thickness of packaged ham. Arrange the ham slices on a wooden board and cut each into 3 strips. Peel the pickle, then, with a potato peeler, cut 12 thin ribbons. First, roll the ribbons up, then fit them to the ham strips; roll both the ham and pickle together, and secure with a toothpick. Dip the ends in chopped parsley or paprika.

EGGPLANT CAVIAR

1 eggplant, about 1–1¼ pounds	*¼ clove garlic, minced*
½ teaspoon salt	*5 scant tablespoons olive oil*
1 tablespoon minced onion	*¾ teaspoon lemon juice*

Preheat oven to 425° F.

Wash eggplant, dry, and place it on a baking sheet. Bake in the preheated oven for about 30–40 minutes, or until soft when pierced with a knife. Split open, cool, then scrape meat from skin onto a chopping board. Chop fine, put into a bowl, and add salt, onion, garlic, oil, and lemon juice. Blend well, refrigerate, and serve with crackers.

CARROT AND NUT SPREAD

2 carrots	*6 ounces ground or broken nuts,*
Mayonnaise	*any variety*
Salt and pepper to taste	*Lemon juice*

Scrape carrots and grate on the coarse side of a household grater. This will make about 1 cup. Add just enough mayonnaise to bind. Season with salt and pepper to taste. Add nuts and a few drops of lemon juice. Refrigerate overnight and serve on crackers.

APPLE AND PEANUT BUTTER SPREAD

2 medium-sized apples of a firm eating variety
1 teaspoon lemon juice
4 tablespoons peanut butter
2 teaspoons mayonnaise

Peel apples, cut into quarters, and remove core. Grate on the coarse side of a household grater. There should be about 2 cups. Sprinkle with lemon juice. Combine peanut butter with mayonnaise and blend into grated apples. Refrigerate before serving. Serve on crackers.

ZUCCHINI WITH SHRIMP

4 baby zucchini
One 7½-ounce can tiny shrimp
1½ tablespoons mayonnaise
1 teaspoon Durkee Famous Sauce
1 teaspoon fresh chopped dill
A few drops of lemon juice
Salt and pepper to taste
Paprika, for garnish

Scrub zucchini and drop them into boiling water; when water returns to the boiling point, remove zucchini and chill. Trim the ends off the zucchini and cut them into 6 or 7 slices about ½ inch thick. With a melon-ball cutter, scoop out the center of each slice, but leave the bottom intact. Drain the shrimp and mash with a fork; add all other ingredients and mix well. Mound the shrimp mixture into the zucchini cups. Dust with paprika and refrigerate before serving.

CHICKEN LIVER PATE

½ pound chicken livers
½ stick butter (2 ounces)
1 cup chopped onion
2 tablespoons flour
1 cup sherry or port wine
One 5-ounce can boned chicken, or
    ¾ cup leftover chicken
    or turkey

5 egg yolks
1 teaspoon salt
½ teaspoon pepper
2 tablespoons chopped parsley
Butter for pan

Preheat oven to 350° F.

Drain chicken livers, pat them dry, and pick them over. Melt the butter, add the onion and sauté until onion softens. Add the chicken livers and sauté until they are just done. Sprinkle flour over the whole, mix, and then add the sherry or port wine. Bring just to the boiling point, then let cool a bit and transfer to a blender and purée. Add the boned chicken and purée some more. Pour into a bowl and add the egg yolks, 1 at a time, beating well. Add salt and pepper and chopped parsley. Butter a bread pan, 9" x 5" x 2½", very well and pour the liver purée into the pan. Place in the preheated oven and bake for 1½ hours, or until loaf is well set. Cool and turn out.

LIVERWURST IN ASPIC

8 ounces liverwurst, about 2–2½
    inches in diameter
1 envelope plain gelatin
One 10½-ounce can beef consommé

½ cup sherry
One 6-inch disposable
    aluminum foil
    loaf pan

Flatten liverwurst slightly so that it will fit the pan. Sprinkle gelatin over the consommé and heat gently until the gelatin is dissolved. Add sherry. Pour enough gelatin liquid into the pan to cover the bottom to a depth of ¼–½ inch. Refrigerate until set. Put liverwurst on top of the gelatin bottom. Pour remaining liquid around and over the liverwurst, and refrigerate. Reserve any remaining liquid, but do not chill it. If liverwurst tends to rise to the surface, wait until the beef consommé begins to set, then push it down and add the remaining liquid. Refrigerate to set. Unmold and serve with crackers.

PART TWO

SOUPS

CREAM OF CARROT SOUP

1 bunch soup greens	*One 12-ounce package frozen*
8 cups water or use 8 cups	*chopped onions*
vegetable stock (see page	*1 teaspoon curry powder*
69)	*1 teaspoon salt*
Two 10-ounce packages frozen	*½ teaspoon pepper*
carrots	*1 cup light cream*

Trim soup greens and cut them up; add odds and ends of lettuce, parsley, or watercress. Put into a stock pot, add water, and simmer for 1 hour. Strain liquid from vegetables, add carrots, onions, curry powder, salt, and pepper to the vegetable broth and simmer until carrots and onions are very soft. Purée the whole in a blender, add cream, and reheat.

VEGETABLE SOUP

Two 13-ounce cans beef broth
Two 14-ounce cans chicken broth, or use homemade beef and chicken stocks in equal proportions, all together 5 cups (see pages 68 and 69)
2 cups water
½ cup grated carrot

½ cup celery, chopped fine
1 cup diced potatoes
1 cup chopped onion
1 cup peeled, chopped tomatoes
2 bay leaves
3 whole peppercorns
2 cups chopped cabbage
Juice of 1 lemon

Combine all the ingredients except the cabbage and lemon juice in a large stew pot and cook at a simmer for 45 minutes. Add cabbage and lemon juice and simmer for 15 minutes more.

SCALLION AND POTATO SOUP

This is a cousin of the well-known *vichyssoise*.

2–3 bunches scallions (about 4 cups sliced)
½ stick butter or margarine (2 ounces)
½ teaspoon nutmeg
2–2½ pounds potatoes

Two 13–14-ounce cans chicken broth, or use 3½–4 cups homemade chicken stock (see page 68)
Milk and yoghurt, or Half & Half

Trim and wash the scallions, and cut both the white and green parts into ½-inch pieces. In a stew pot, melt the butter or margarine and add scallions and nutmeg. Sauté over low heat until the scallions are soft. Peel, slice, and wash potatoes; add to scallions along with the stock. Simmer until potatoes are very soft. Press through a food mill and discard fibrous matter. Dilute with milk, or milk and yoghurt or Half & Half to the desired consistency. Reheat or serve cold.

BEAN SOUP

2 cups navy beans	*1 cup chopped onion*
6 cups ham stock (see page 70)	*½ cup chopped celery*
2 cups tomato juice	*Salt and pepper to taste*

Soak beans overnight, drain, and combine with all other ingredients. Simmer for 2½–3 hours, or until beans are soft. Cool and refrigerate. Reheat the next day and taste for seasoning. Saltiness will depend upon the flavoring of the ham stock.

GREEN SPLIT PEA SOUP

1½ cups green split peas	*Croutons or bacon, for garnish*
7½–8 cups ham stock (see page 70)	*1 small potato, peeled and sliced thin (optional)*
Salt and pepper to taste	

Wash split peas and pick them over. Combine peas and stock and simmer for 1–1½ hours, until peas fall to pieces. Season with salt and pepper to taste. If a thicker soup is desired, add potatoes in the last half-hour. Put the whole mixture through a food mill, refrigerate, and reheat the next day. Garnish with croutons or bits of crisp bacon.

LENTIL SOUP

1 pound lentils
1 large onion, stuck with a clove
1 bay leaf
8 cups ham stock (see page 70)
1/2 stick butter or margarine (2 ounces)

3 tablespoons flour
Salt and pepper to taste
3 tablespoons vinegar (optional)
3–4 frankfurters, for garnish

Combine lentils, onion, bay leaf, and ham stock and simmer until lentils are soft, about 2 hours. Remove bay leaf and onion. Melt the butter or margarine, add flour and brown lightly; add to soup as a thickener, taste for salt and pepper, and add vinegar if desired. A garnish of sliced frankfurters heated in the soup is customary.

CREAM OF LETTUCE SOUP

4 cups shredded lettuce. Use very dark green leaves, such as the outer leaves of romaine, Boston, or escarole.
5 cups chicken stock, homemade (see page 68) or canned
2 slices of onion

1 potato, chopped coarse or shredded
1/4 teaspoon nutmeg
Salt and pepper to taste
Half & Half
Croutons or chopped parsley, for garnish

Combine shredded lettuce, chicken stock, onion, potato, nutmeg and simmer for a half-hour. Taste for seasoning. Continue simmering until potatoes fall to pieces. Put in a blender and purée. Refrigerate overnight. Next day, reheat and thin out with Half & Half. Serve with croutons or chopped parsley.

CREAM OF CUCUMBER SOUP

4 medium-sized cucumbers	½ cup Half & Half
½ stick butter (2 ounces)	1 tablespoon cornstarch
3 slices of onion	Salt and pepper to taste
4 cups chicken stock, homemade (see page 68) or canned	2 tablespoons chopped fresh dill, for garnish

Peel cucumbers, cut in half lengthwise and scrape seeds out with a spoon; dice cucumbers. In a saucepan, melt the butter, add onions and sauté until soft; add cucumbers and sauté a little bit longer. Then add chicken stock and simmer for 30 minutes. Put the whole into a blender and purée; return to a saucepan to cool and refrigerate overnight. Combine Half & Half with cornstarch, add to the cucumber purée, and reheat until the soup is slightly thickened. Taste for seasoning and serve garnished with chopped dill.

WHITE POTATO SOUP

6 potatoes, peeled and sliced	1 quart milk (4 cups)
4 ribs of celery with tops, diced	1 cup light cream
1 large onion, sliced	2 tablespoons butter or margarine
1 teaspoon salt	Salt and pepper to taste

Combine the potatoes, celery, and onion in a pot and cover with water. Simmer until vegetables are soft. Drain and place in a blender. Add 2 cups of the milk and purée. Return to saucepan and add 2 more cups of milk, bring to the boiling point, then cool and refrigerate. Next day, reheat, add cream, butter, and taste for seasoning. Thin with more milk if desired.

RICH VEGETABLE SOUP

½ cup dry white beans
4 cups vegetable stock (see page 69)
2 tablespoons butter or margarine
1 pound ground beef
½ cup elbow macaroni

One 16-ounce can peeled tomatoes
½ cup diced celery
1 cup diced carrots
1 cup chopped onion

Soak beans overnight; drain, combine with vegetable stock, and simmer until beans begin to get soft, about a half-hour. Melt the butter or margarine, add the ground beef and cook until lightly browned; add to the soup along with the elbow macaroni, tomatoes, diced celery, carrots, and onion. Simmer for 30 minutes, then cool and refrigerate. Next day, reheat and simmer until vegetables are soft.

BASIC CHICKEN STOCK

Use either the carcasses from 4 broiler/fryers (see Note), or use 4 pounds of chicken backs.

2 cups soup greens, or use trimmings from
    parsley, parsley stems, 2 or 3 carrots, lettuce leaves, and celery tops and outer ribs
2 onions, stuck with 2 cloves each

3 quarts water
1 bay leaf
8 peppercorns
2 tablespoons salt

Combine all the ingredients in a large stock pot, about 2 or 3 gallons, and simmer for 4 hours. Drain, discard bones, vegetables, and spices; cool and refrigerate. Next day, scrape off all fat.

NOTE:
It is more economical to buy the whole broiler/fryers than the parts. Use boneless, skinless breast of chicken for Chicken Breasts in Curry

Sauce and Pineapple (see page 165), or Chicken with Ham and Cheese (see page 154), and use the legs for Baked Chicken Legs (see page 24–25). Of course, both boneless breasts and legs can also be frozen for future use.

BASIC BEEF STOCK

4 pounds beef bones, preferably with some meat,   *3 quarts water*
     if not, add ½ pound stewing beef   *2 bay leaves*
2 cups soup greens, or use trimmings from celery,   *10 peppercorns*
     lettuce, tomatoes, a few carrots, and 3   *2 tablespoons salt*
     onions, each stuck with a clove

Combine all the ingredients in a large stock pot and simmer for 4 hours. Drain and discard all vegetables and bones. Cool and refrigerate overnight; remove fat the next day.

VEGETABLE STOCK

This can be the most economical of all stocks. Place all trimmings, such as peels from carrots, parsnips, potatoes, celery tops and outer ribs, tomatoes, lettuce, stems from parsley and watercress, and scallions into a plastic bag and keep them in the freezer, adding new trimmings as you go along. When you have accumulated 4 or 5 cups of trimmings, put them into a pot, add 7 or 8 cups of water, a tablespoon of salt and, if it is available, a white turnip or parsnip. Bring to the boiling point and simmer for about 1 hour, then strain, cool, and chill, and use as directed. This vegetable stock can be used, for example, with canned chicken or beef stock instead of water. If desired, vegetable stock may be frozen in a plastic container.

HAM STOCK

1 ham bone or 1½–2 pounds smoked pork hocks	*1 carrot, scraped*
	1 cup parsley stems
3 quarts water	*1 onion, stuck with 2 cloves*
1 parsnip, scraped	*1 bay leaf*

If you don't have a ham bone or the bone from any other smoked pork, use the pork hocks. Combine all the ingredients, bring to the boiling point, and simmer for 2–3 hours. Drain liquid off and discard vegetables. Pick the meat off the hocks and discard bones and skin. Refrigerate broth and remove fat before using. This stock can be used as the base for any pea, bean, or legume soup.

PART TWO

MEAT AND POULTRY

NEW ENGLAND AUTUMN STEW

2½–3 pounds beef chuck, cut for
    stew
2 cups chopped onion, about 1
    large
2 cups sliced carrots, about 4
    large
2 cups parsnips, about 3 large,
    diced

2 cups white turnips, about 6,
    diced
¼ teaspoon each of dried rose-
    mary, basil, and marjoram
2 cups water
2 beef bouillon cubes

In a large stew pot, combine meat, onion, carrots, parsnips, turnips, and seasonings. Combine water and bouillon cubes and heat until cubes are dissolved; then add to the other ingredients. Simmer for 1½ hours and test meat for doneness. Continue cooking if necessary until meat is fork tender.

GOULASH

2½–3 pounds cubed beef chuck
2 tablespoons margarine or vege-
    table oil
2 cups chopped onion
Two 16-ounce cans peeled toma-
    toes

4 green peppers, free of ribs and
    seeds, cut into strips
1 tablespoon paprika
1 teaspoon salt
½ teaspoon pepper

Rinse meat and pat dry. Melt the margarine or oil, add onion and sauté for a few minutes; then add meat, tomatoes, and green pepper strips. Blend paprika into the liquid and add salt and pepper. Simmer over low heat for about 1½–2 hours, or until meat is fork tender. Stir occasionally. If stew gets too dry, add a bit of water.

BEEF STEW AND POTATOES

2½–3 pounds cubed beef chuck
3 tablespoons margarine or vegetable oil
4 onions, chopped, about 3 cups
½ clove garlic, chopped very fine
Beef stock, homemade (see page 69),
    canned, or made with dissolved
    bouillon cubes

1 tablespoon paprika
Salt and pepper to taste
1 teaspoon caraway seeds
3 cups diced raw potatoes

Rinse meat and pat dry. Melt the margarine or oil and sear the meat lightly; add onions and sauté, but do not brown; add garlic and enough meat stock to cover the meat and onions. Blend paprika into the liquid, add salt and pepper and caraway seeds, and simmer for 30–45 minutes, until meat begins to get soft; then add the potatoes. Continue cooking until meat and potatoes are done.

SZEGEDINER GULYAS

1½ pounds pork, cut into 1½-
    inch cubes
1½ pounds beef chuck, cut into
    1½-inch cubes
2 cups onions, sliced thin
4 tablespoons margarine or vege-
    table oil

2 teaspoons paprika
¼ teaspoon ground allspice
1 teaspoon salt
1 pound cooked sauerkraut

Rinse meat and pat dry. Sauté onions in the fat, add cubed meat, and sear well on all sides. Add paprika, allspice, and salt, and cook for 15 minutes, stirring occasionally. Add sauerkraut and cook 30–45 minutes longer, until meat is fork tender. Serve with noodles.

DILL LAMB

4–6 lamb shanks
2 carrots
2 leeks
1 bunch fresh dill
2 teaspoons whole peppercorns

2 teaspoons salt
8 tablespoons butter
8 tablespoons flour
1 tablespoon lemon juice

Rinse lamb shanks and put into a stew pot. Scrape carrots and cut into 1-inch pieces. Wash leeks very well and cut into 1-inch pieces. Cut the stems from the dill and wash; reserve the dill leaves. Add carrots, leeks, and dill stems to lamb shanks. Cover with water and add peppercorns and salt. Bring to the boiling point and simmer until meat is tender, about 1½–2 hours. Cool and refrigerate overnight. Remove fat, cut meat off the bones, and cube. Discard vegetables. Melt the butter, add flour and blend; to this mixture add 4 cups of the lamb cooking liquid and simmer for a while. Add cubed meat and reheat. Add lemon juice.

Chop reserved dill leaves. When meat is heated through, turn off heat and add chopped dill. Do not boil again.

JULIA'S PUERTO RICAN BEEF STEW

This recipe was given to me by my friend Julia Polanco.

2 tablespoons olive oil	6 ribs of celery, sliced
3 pounds cubed beef chuck	12 stuffed green olives, cut in half
2 medium-sized onions, sliced	4 ounces tomato sauce
2 tablespoons flour	4 beef bouillon cubes
1 teaspoon garlic powder	2 cups water
½ teaspoon oregano	4 medium-sized potatoes, peeled and
½ teaspoon pepper	quartered
6 carrots, sliced	

In a stew pot, heat the olive oil, add the beef cubes and onions, sprinkle with flour, and brown a little bit. Then add garlic powder, oregano, pepper, carrots, and celery and brown some more. Add olives and tomato sauce, stir well, and lower heat to a simmer. Dissolve bouillon cubes in water and add to the stew. Cover pot and simmer for about 1–1½ hours. When meat is almost done, remove from heat and refrigerate.

Next day, reheat, add potatoes, and cook until potatoes and meat are fork tender. If potatoes have not thickened the stew sufficiently, add a little bit more flour mixed with water. If desired, add cooked green peas and/or cooked green beans.

OXTAIL RAGOUT

5 pounds oxtail, cut into pieces	*2 cups red wine*
Flour	*1 bay leaf*
Butter or margarine, as needed	*½ teaspoon thyme*
4 onions, chopped coarse	*½ teaspoon ground ginger*
3 carrots, chopped	*2 teaspoons salt*
2 white turnips, chopped	*1 teaspoon pepper*
One 14-ounce can beef broth, or use	*2 ounces brandy*
* homemade stock (see page 69)*	

Rinse oxtail pieces and pat dry. Roll in flour and brown in butter or margarine a few pieces at a time. Place in a stew pot along with the chopped onions, carrots, turnips, beef broth, and wine. If necessary, add just enough water to cover all. Add bay leaf, thyme, ginger, salt, and pepper, and simmer for 2½–3 hours, until oxtails are tender. Remove from heat and refrigerate. Take off fat and reheat the quite gelatinous mixture. Remove oxtails and fish out bay leaf. Purée the sauce in a blender or put it through a food mill. Return to the pot, add meat pieces and brandy. Taste for seasoning and reheat.

IRISH STEW

3–4 pounds lamb shoulder	*3 white turnips*
1 large onion, stuck with 3 cloves	*2 leeks*
1 bay leaf	*3 large onions*
1 teaspoon thyme	*4 or 5 large potatoes, diced (about*
3 carrots	* 4 cups)*

It will take about 2 days to prepare a lean stew.

Have your butcher bone the lamb shoulder and request the bones. Wash the bones and put them into a large kettle with water to cover;

add the onion stuck with cloves and the bay leaf; simmer for 1½ hours. Strain off liquid and refrigerate. Remove fat. Cut meat into 1½-inch cubes and put into a stew pot. Scrape carrots, peel turnips, and cut both into cubes. Wash leeks very well and cut into 1-inch pieces. Peel and slice onions. Add all the vegetables to the meat and pour bone cooking liquid over the whole. Simmer for 45 minutes, then test for doneness; continue to simmer until meat is almost done. Remove from heat and refrigerate. Remove fat, add potatoes, and simmer until meat is fork tender and potatoes are well done. The potatoes will thicken the broth.

GREEK LAMB STEW

This is a recipe from Thalia Sophia Daratsakis Mazurek, from her mother's recipe book.

3 pounds boneless stewing lamb, cut into ¾-inch cubes	*Two 4-ounce cans tomato paste*
	3 cups water
2 tablespoons butter or margarine	*1½ cups white wine*
2 tablespoons olive oil	*Salt and pepper to taste*
2 large onions, chopped	*2 tablespoons chopped parsley*
1 clove garlic, chopped	

Rinse meat and pat dry. In a casserole with a lid, melt the butter or margarine, add oil, and turn heat low; add onions and garlic and sauté until onions begin to get transparent. Add meat and brown all over, keeping heat low; then add tomato paste, water, and wine and stir well. Bring to the boiling point, reduce heat to a simmer, cover, and cook for about 1–1¼ hours. Cool and refrigerate. Next day, reheat, taste for seasoning, and simmer, covered, for another 30 minutes. Sprinkle with parsley and serve directly from the casserole.

VARIATIONS:
Add vegetables such as okra, green beans, or peas.

CURRIED CHICKEN OR TURKEY PARTS

6 chicken legs and thighs, or use 6 small turkey drumsticks or thighs
4 large onions
1 tablespoon curry powder
1 teaspoon salt

Rinse chicken or turkey pieces and place in a stew pot. Slice onions and cut slices in half; add onions with curry powder and salt to the meat along with enough water to cover. Simmer until meat is done, about 1–1½ hours. Remove meat, put cooking liquid into a blender, and purée. If this sauce is too thin, reduce over high heat to a creamy consistency. Return meat to sauce, refrigerate, and reheat the following day.

PORTUGUESE PORK STEW

5–6 pounds pork shoulder, *1 teaspoon pepper*
cubed *1 lemon*
2 cups white wine or dry vermouth *3 tablespoons chopped coriander*
2 teaspoons ground cumin *or parsley*
2 teaspoons salt

Have your butcher bone the pork shoulder and cube the meat. Cut off as much fat as possible, and reserve about 2 tablespoons in which to brown the meat. Add 1½ cups of the wine or vermouth, the cumin, salt, and pepper to the browned meat, and simmer until it is fork tender. Remove from the heat and refrigerate. Remove fat and reheat. Slice the lemon thin, and cut each slice into quarters and add to the stew along with the remaining ½ cup wine or vermouth. Simmer for another 15–20 minutes, then add the coriander or parsley.

BEEF STEWED WITH BEER

3 pounds beef chuck, cut into 1–1½-inch cubes	1 cup diced carrots
2 tablespoons butter or margarine	2 cups beer
2 cups diced onion	1 tablespoon paprika
One 16-ounce can peeled tomatoes	Salt and pepper to taste
	2 cups diced potatoes

In a frying pan, brown beef cubes in butter or margarine and place in a 2-quart saucepan with a lid. Add onions, tomatoes, carrots, and beer; sprinkle paprika over all and blend. Simmer, covered, for 1–1½ hours, until meat is almost done, then taste for seasoning. Cool and refrigerate. Next day, reheat, add potatoes, and simmer for another 20 minutes or so, until potatoes are done.

LAMB STEW WITH ONIONS AND CARAWAY SEED

3 pounds boneless stewing lamb	1 teaspoon caraway seeds
4 cups vegetable stock (see page 69)	3 tablespoons butter or margarine
	4 tablespoons flour
4 cups sliced onions (about 4 large)	Salt and pepper to taste

Combine lamb and vegetable stock and simmer until lamb is done, about 1½ hours. Cool and refrigerate. Next day, remove fat, drain stock from lamb into a saucepan, add onions and caraway seeds, and simmer until onions are soft, about a half-hour. Melt the butter or margarine and blend in flour. Add some of the cooking liquid to the butter/flour mixture, blend and stir to dissolve; then add to the meat and onions, taste for seasoning, and reheat for 15 minutes.

BEEF AND KIDNEY STEW

2 pounds beef chuck, cut into 1-inch
    pieces
1 veal kidney, about 1 pound, without
    fat, cubed
4 tablespoons flour
6 tablespoons butter or margarine
1 medium-sized onion, sliced medium
    thick and slices cut into quarters

1/2 pound fresh mushrooms,
    washed and sliced
1 cup water
3/4 cup red wine
1/4 teaspoon thyme
1/4 teaspoon marjoram
Salt and pepper to taste

Rinse beef pieces and pat them dry; cut kidney in half, remove ducts, and cut into 1-inch cubes. Combine beef and kidney pieces and dust with flour. In a frying pan melt 5 tablespoons of the butter or margarine and brown meat pieces a few at a time. Put the browned pieces into a casserole with a lid. When all meat pieces are browned, add the remaining tablespoon of fat to the frying pan and sauté the onions; then add mushrooms and sauté for about 3 minutes longer. Add onions and mushrooms to meat pieces. Add water to frying pan, simmer, and scrape the bottom to loosen all brown particles. Then add this mixture to meat along with the wine, thyme, and marjoram. Season with salt and pepper to taste, bring the whole to the boiling point, and reduce heat to a simmer. Cover and cook for about 1–1 1/2 hours, then check for doneness. If necessary, continue simmering until meat is fork tender. Cool and refrigerate. Next day, reheat for about 15 minutes and serve directly from the casserole. If desired, thicken sauce with a bit of cornstarch.

AUSTRIAN HUNTERS STEW

3 pounds veal shoulder, cut into
    1-inch cubes
2 tablespoons flour
6 slices of bacon
1 large onion, chopped
1 clove garlic, minced
3 carrots, scraped and cut into
    strips

2 green peppers, seeded and cut
    into strips
2 cups water
6 tablespoons wine vinegar
1 cup beef stock, homemade (see
    page 69) or canned
1 cup uncooked white rice
Salt and pepper to taste

Rinse meat, pat dry, and roll in flour; set aside. Cut bacon into ¼-inch pieces and fry until crisp. Remove the bacon pieces and set aside. Pour off all but 1½ tablespoons of bacon fat; add onions and garlic and sauté until onions begin to get transparent. Then add carrot and green pepper strips, and cook for about 5 minutes; add the floured meat and cook another few minutes, stirring all the time to brown evenly. Add water and vinegar, bacon strips, and simmer for about 30 minutes, or until meat begins to get tender. Cool and refrigerate overnight.

Next day, add beef stock and rice, cover, and simmer for 15 minutes. If more liquid is needed, add water. Taste for seasoning and simmer until meat and rice are done, adding more water if necessary. The dish should be moist but not soupy.

SMOKED TONGUE

1 smoked beef tongue, 3–4½
    pounds
1 large onion, stuck with 4 cloves

1 bay leaf
2 sprigs parsley
1 outer rib of celery with leaves

Put tongue into a large kettle, add onion stuck with cloves, bay leaf, parsley, celery and cover well with water. The water should stand at least 2 inches above the tongue. Bring to the boiling point and reduce heat to a simmer. Remove any scum that forms on the surface. Continue simmering until the tip of the tongue can be pierced easily with a fork, about 40–50 minutes per pound. Remove tongue from liquid and let cool just enough to handle. Remove skin and cut off root end, remove all meat from the cut-off pieces, and use them for a spread. If desired, cut off tip of tongue and add to the salvaged meat. Put tongue back into cooking liquid and refrigerate. Reheat before slicing very thin. Serve with a raisin or mustard sauce (see below).

RAISIN SAUCE

1 cup seedless raisins   *½ cup tongue cooking liquid (see page 80–81)*
2 cups red wine   *¼ teaspoon dry mustard*
3 tablespoons butter   *⅛ teaspoon mace*
3 tablespoons flour   *Salt and pepper to taste*

Put seedless raisins into a bowl, add ½ cup of the red wine, and let stand for about a half-hour. Melt the butter, add flour and blend well; then add the remaining red wine and the cooking liquid. Stir until smooth. Add raisins and their liquid, mustard, mace, salt and pepper, and simmer for 15–20 minutes. Keep warm or reheat in a water bath or double boiler before serving.

MUSTARD SAUCE

3 tablespoons butter   *1 cup tongue cooking liquid (see page 80–81)*
3 tablespoons flour   *2 tablespoons prepared mustard, either Dijon or*
½ cup light cream   *Düsseldorf*
Salt and pepper to taste

Melt the butter, add flour and blend. Beat in the light cream and the tongue cooking liquid; blend well. Add mustard, simmer, and taste for seasoning. This will make a sharp sauce. For a milder flavor, reduce the amount of mustard.

BAKED SHORT RIBS OF BEEF

16 small or 8 large beef ribs　　*Salt and pepper to taste*
One 10-ounce package frozen　　*One 16-ounce can peeled toma-*
　　chopped onions　　　　　　　*toes*

Preheat oven to 375° F.

Rinse ribs in water and pat them dry to remove all bone splinters. Select a covered baking dish large enough to hold ribs in a single layer. Spread half the onions over the bottom of the dish, arrange ribs on top, then add the remaining onions and season to taste. Pour the tomatoes over all, cover, and bake in the preheated oven for 1½–2 hours, or until the ribs are fork tender. Cool and refrigerate. Next day, remove fat and reheat for 15–20 minutes in a 375° F. oven.

ROULADEN

6 slices of top round steak, each　*4 tablespoons butter or margarine*
　about ½ inch thick　　　　　*2½–3 cups vegetable stock (see*
Mustard　　　　　　　　　　　　*page 69) or water*
6 slices of bacon　　　　　　　*2 tablespoons butter*
6 tablespoons chopped onion　　*2 tablespoons flour*
1 large dill pickle　　　　　　*Salt and pepper to taste*

Pound the slices of beef to about ¼ inch thick, 4 inches wide, and 7–8 inches long. (These pounded slices are sometimes available in the meat market labeled *bracioli,* the Italian version of Rouladen.) Line up slices and spread them with mustard. Put a slice of bacon on each meat slice and spread with a tablespoon of onion. Cut the dill pickle into 6 strips and put 1 strip at the end of each meat slice. Now, roll up the meat, starting at the end where the pickle is, and secure each roll with kitchen string or toothpicks. In a saucepan with a lid, melt the 4 tablespoons butter or margarine, and brown the beef rolls on all sides. Add the vegetable stock or water and simmer for 1–1½ hours, until the meat is fork tender. Cool and refrigerate. Next day, melt 2 tablespoons butter in a frying pan, add 2 tablespoons flour, blend, and add the liquid from the beef rolls, stirring constantly; bring to the boiling point. Pour over the Rouladen and reheat for 15–20 minutes.

STUFFED CABBAGE

1 large head cabbage	*Grated peel of 1 lemon*
1 pound ground veal	*Salt and pepper to taste*
1 pound ground beef	*¼ teaspoon nutmeg*
1 cup chopped onion	*Bacon slices*
6 slices of white bread	*½ cup water or beef stock, homemade*
6 tablespoons Half & Half	*(see page 69) or canned*
3 eggs	

Preheat oven to 300° F.

Remove the core, as completely as possible, from the cabbage. Drop the whole head into boiling salted water and cook for 7–8 minutes, then remove and carefully peel off as many whole leaves as possible. Repeat, boiling cabbage head and again peeling off the leaves. Pat the detached leaves dry and arrange on a board with 2 large leaves and some smaller ones in the middle. Make 12 piles. Save cabbage leaves too small to use for soup. In a large bowl combine veal, beef, and onion. Trim bread slices, discard crusts, and crumble centers. Moisten with Half & Half and add to meat, along with the eggs, lemon peel, salt, pepper, and nutmeg. Using your hands, combine all ingredients, squeezing them through your fingers. Divide the meat mixture among the cabbage piles and roll up, tucking in the sides. Line a baking dish large enough to hold the cabbage rolls with bacon strips. Arrange cabbage rolls on top, seam side down, add water or beef stock, and bake in the preheated oven for 2 hours, basting every half-hour with the liquid in the dish. Cool and refrigerate. Next day, reheat for 30 minutes in a 300° F. oven.

CORNED BEEF AND CABBAGE

3–4 pounds corned beef. Use either the thin cut, which is rather lean, or the thick cut, which is streaked with layers of fat.

1 onion, stuck with a clove
1 bay leaf
2 small, tight heads cabbage, quartered

Wipe corned beef, put it into a kettle, add water to cover, and bring to the boiling point. Remove scum. Simmer for a half-hour and taste water. If very salty, discard first water and cover with fresh. Add onion and bay leaf, and continue simmering for 2–3 hours. Test meat for doneness; if necessary, continue to simmer for another half-hour until meat is fork tender. It is very difficult to predict how long to cook corned beef because the quality of the meat varies. Cool and refrigerate in the cooking broth. Next day, reheat and simmer for another 15 minutes, remove meat, and keep warm. To the broth add the quartered cabbage and cook for 15 minutes. Serve sliced meat surrounded by cabbage with mustard or horseradish and parsley potatoes.

BAKED PORK CHOPS

6 center-cut pork chops, each
    about 1 inch thick
½ teaspoon each ground sage and
    rosemary
½ clove garlic, minced
1 teaspoon salt

½ teaspoon pepper
2 tablespoons butter or margarine
2 tablespoons olive oil
1 cup white wine
2 tablespoons chopped parsley,
    for garnish

Wipe pork chops with a damp cloth and arrange on waxed paper. Combine ground sage and rosemary with the minced garlic, salt, and pepper. Divide half this mixture among the 6 chops. Cover with waxed paper and pound the seasoning into the meat. Turn the chops and repeat on the other side. In a frying pan, melt the butter or margarine, add olive oil and brown the chops well on both sides. Arrange in a single layer in a baking dish, pour off fat from the frying pan, add wine and let simmer for a while, scraping the bottom to loosen brown particles. Pour over pork chops, cool, and refrigerate. Next day, preheat oven to 350° F., cover the baking dish with aluminum foil, and bake chops for 30–45 minutes, until they are fork tender. Serve directly from the baking dish, garnished with chopped parsley.

CHICKEN FRICASSEE

2 chickens, broiler/fryers, 2½–3 pounds
    each
4–5 cups water or vegetable stock (see
    page 69)
1 onion, stuck with a clove
1 teaspoon salt

3–4 peppercorns
1 bay leaf
6 tablespoons chicken fat
6 tablespoons flour
Juice of 1 lemon

Usually stewing fowl are used for chicken fricassee, but stewing fowl are rare on the market these days, so younger chickens are substituted in this recipe. Rinse chickens, reserve livers for other purposes, but use the gizzards. In a stew pot cover the chickens with water or vegetable stock. Add onion, salt, peppercorns, and bay leaf. Simmer slowly for about 45 minutes; then remove chickens, cut off breasts, legs, and wings, remove oysters on the back, cool a bit, then remove skin from all parts and return to stock together with stripped carcasses. Simmer stock for another 30 minutes. Divide legs into thighs and drumsticks. Cut breasts in half. Cut off wing tip from wings. Put all pieces into a bowl and strain cooking liquid over them. Discard bones, bay leaf, and onion; cool and refrigerate.

Next day, take off 6 tablespoons chicken fat and discard the rest. Melt the fat, add the 6 tablespoons flour and blend; then add 3 cups of the chicken cooking liquid and, while stirring constantly, bring to the boiling point. Add chicken pieces and reheat for 15 minutes. Turn off heat and add lemon juice.

VARIATIONS:
Add any or all—canned finger-sized carrots, small green peas, asparagus tips.

SWISS STEAK

2½–3 pounds round steak, sliced	*2 tablespoons butter or margarine*
about 1½–2 inches thick	*2 tablespoons oil*
1 clove garlic, split	*1 cup onion, sliced thin*
⅓ cup flour	*1 cup red wine*
2 teaspoons salt	*Beef stock, as needed, homemade*
1 teaspoon dried thyme	*(see page 69) or canned*
½ teaspoon pepper	*4 tablespoons chopped parsley*

Wipe the meat with a damp cloth and rub it with garlic on both sides. Combine flour, salt, thyme, and pepper; sprinkle half over meat and pound the seasonings in with a meat-tenderizer hammer or any other heavy utensil. Turn meat and treat the other side the same way. Melt the butter or margarine in a frying pan with a lid, add oil and brown meat well on both sides; add onions and sauté until transparent. Add wine and enough stock to about half cover the meat. Cover the pan and simmer for 1 hour. Cool and refrigerate.

Next day, preheat oven to 350° F. Transfer meat to an ovenproof casserole, pour the liquid over, and bake in the preheated oven for 35–40 minutes. If there is not enough liquid add more wine. When meat is done, remove to a platter and slice. If desired, thicken the sauce with a bit of cornstarch, or reduce over high heat to a creamy consistency. Add parsley just before serving.

BAKED SMOKED PORK SHOULDER

1 smoked pork shoulder, with bone, about 5–6 pounds
1¼ tablespoons dry mustard

¾ cup apricot butter or marmalade
1½ ounces brandy
Whole cloves, for garnish

Put pork shoulder into a stock pot and cover with water. Simmer for 2 hours, cool, and refrigerate in the broth. Next day, preheat oven to 325° F. Remove skin from shoulder and place meat, fat side up, in a roasting pan. Reheat meat for 45 minutes, remove from oven, and turn temperature up to 400° F. Blend together dry mustard and apricot butter or marmalade; add the brandy. Score the fat in a square pattern; then spread the mustard mixture over all and garnish with whole cloves stuck in the centers of the squares. Put 1 cup water into the pan and bake for 10–15 minutes, until the glaze is brown. Cool for 30 minutes before slicing.

NOTE:
Save stock, bone, and skin for ham stock.

PORK AND RICE CASSEROLE

4–5 pounds pork shoulder, boned and cut into 1-inch pieces
½ cup butter or margarine
2 onions, sliced thin
1 tablespoon paprika

1 teaspoon salt
5 cups chicken or vegetable stock (see page 68–69)
1 cup uncooked white rice
¾ cup grated Parmesan cheese

Rinse the meat and pat dry. Melt the butter or margarine, add sliced onion and sauté until light yellow. Add meat cubes and sear them lightly, but do not brown. Add paprika, salt, and stock to about half cover the meat. Cover the pot and cook for 30 minutes over low heat on top of the stove, or in a 350° F. oven. Cool and refrigerate.

Next day, add rice and remainder of the stock, stir, cover, and cook for 30 minutes longer. Check the amount of liquid absorbed by the rice and add water if needed. There should be some liquid left after the rice is cooked, although the dish should not be soupy. When rice and meat are done, sprinkle the whole with grated cheese and serve.

ZRAZI

2 pounds ground beef
3 eggs
8 slices of white bread, crumbled
    and moistened with water,
    then pressed dry
1 teaspoon salt
1 teaspoon pepper

1 jar prepared white horseradish,
    drained and pressed dry
Butter
2 tablespoons flour
1½ cups beef stock, homemade
    (see page 69) or canned

Mix the ground beef, eggs, bread crumbs, and seasonings. When well blended, divide evenly to make 12 patties. Press each patty out flat and cover with about 2 teaspoons pressed-out horseradish. Roll up like a sausage and pinch ends together to seal. Brown the meat in butter in a pan. When well browned, sprinkle with flour, add stock, cover, cool, and refrigerate. Next day, preheat oven to 325° F. and bake Zrazi rolls for about a half-hour.

SHEPHERD'S PIE

This is a great supper dish, perfect for using up leftover lamb and gravy. Should there not be enough leftover lamb, some ground lamb may be added, and if not enough gravy, peeled canned tomatoes will be helpful.

3 pounds leftover lamb, or add
    enough raw ground lamb
    as needed, or use all raw
    ground lamb
3 tablespoons butter or margarine
3 cups chopped onion
1 bay leaf

2 teaspoons prepared mustard
1 teaspoon dried thyme
1 cup lamb gravy, or use one 8-
    ounce can peeled tomatoes
2½ pounds potatoes
2½ cups milk
2 tablespoons butter

Grind roast lamb and put it into a bowl, add raw ground lamb if needed, or use all raw ground lamb. Melt the butter, add onions and sauté until they are wilted. Add meat and cook, breaking up lumps if any; add bay leaf, mustard, and thyme; add gravy or drain tomatoes over the meat, chop up pulp, then add to the meat. Stir well. The mixture should be moist but not soupy; water may be added if needed. Pour into a baking dish, about 9″ x 15″ x 2″, or of similar proportions. Cool and refrigerate.

Next day, peel potatoes, cut them into small pieces, cover with salted water, and boil until very soft, about 20–25 minutes. Press them through a food mill. Heat milk, add to potatoes along with the 2 tablespoons of butter and make mashed potatoes. Spread over lamb in baking dish and smooth out. Preheat oven to 400° F. and bake Shepherd's Pie in the preheated oven for 25–30 minutes.

NOTE:
If desired, complete the Shepherd's Pie, including the potatoes, the night before, then just reheat before serving.

STUFFED CORNISH HENS

3 Cornish hens	*½ cup dry bread crumbs*
1 pound ground veal	*2 eggs*
½ pound fresh mushrooms, rinsed and	*6 strips of bacon*
chopped	*1 cup red wine*
1 onion, chopped	*6 tablespoons fat*
½ teaspoon dried tarragon	*Butter or margarine*
1 teaspoon salt	*6 tablespoons flour*
½ teaspoon pepper	*Red wine and water for sauce*

Preheat oven to 350° F.

Cut Cornish hens in half lengthwise, rinse, and pat dry. Chop and reserve the livers and use the neck and gizzards for other purposes. Put ground veal into a bowl. Add chopped livers, mushrooms, onions, tarragon, salt, pepper, bread crumbs, and eggs. Mix all together with your hands, squeezing through your fingers. Divide into 6 equal parts and stuff the Cornish hens with the mixture. Put a strip of bacon over the stuffing and arrange the hens, stuffed side up, in a baking dish in a single layer. Add wine and bake for 45 minutes in the preheated oven. Remove from oven, cool, and refrigerate.

Next day, preheat oven to 350° F., remove hens from pan, and scrape off all fat. Discard the bacon strips. Measure the fat and add enough butter or margarine to make 6 tablespoons. Blend in the 6 tablespoons of flour. Measure cooking liquid from hens and add enough wine and water to make 3 cups. Add this to the flour mixture and stir well; cook for 5 minutes. Arrange hens in a baking dish, stuffed side down, cover with some of the sauce, and reheat for 30 minutes in the 350° F. oven. Keep remaining sauce hot and serve on the side. Serve the hens directly from the baking dish.

BAKED LAMB CHOPS

6 shoulder lamb chops, or lamb steaks, each 1½ inches thick	½ teaspoon dried basil
	½ teaspoon dried thyme
1 tablespoon oil	½ teaspoon pepper
2 large onions, sliced	6 anchovy fillets
3 large or 6 small tomatoes, sliced	

Wipe lamb chops or lamb steaks and trim off fat along the edges. Chop the fat and render over low heat in a frying pan. Brown meat on both sides in this fat. Remove meat to a platter, add oil to pan, and sauté the onions until they are transparent. Add the tomatoes to the pan, together with the basil, thyme, and pepper. Simmer for a few minutes, then cool. Pour into a blender, add anchovies, and purée. Arrange the lamb chops or steaks in an overlapping layer in a baking dish; pour vegetable purée over meat. Refrigerate. Next day, preheat oven to 375° F., and bake chops or steaks for about 35 minutes, or until meat is fork tender. Serve directly from the baking dish.

PART TWO

VEGETABLES

RATATOUILLE

The best ratatouille I ever made was in a cottage near Hungerford, England, when all the ingredients, except the garlic, came from the vegetable patch.

Garlic is a basic ingredient of ratatouille in the *Provençal* manner, but if you are not a garlic lover it will not be a disaster if you omit it.

¾ cup olive oil
2 medium-sized onions, about
    2 cups, chopped
2 cloves garlic, chopped
    (optional)
1 large zucchini, or green squash,
    diced fine

2 green peppers, diced
1 large eggplant, peeled and diced
10–12 very ripe tomatoes
1 teaspoon salt
½ teaspoon pepper

In a large frying pan, combine olive oil, onions, and garlic and sauté until onions begin to get soft. Add zucchini, peppers, and eggplant, mix well, and cook for about 10 minutes over low heat. Add the tomatoes, salt, and pepper and stir. Cover and cook for 15 minutes; then remove cover and, while stirring gently, reduce the liquid from the vegetables. Do not cook to a mush, as is advised in many recipes. Taste for seasoning, then either serve immediately or refrigerate and reheat the next day. Any leftovers can be served as a salad course.

CREAMED POTATOES AU GRATIN

1½ cups Half & Half	½ teaspoon nutmeg
½ bay leaf	½ teaspoon pepper
2 slices of onion	½ teaspoon salt
6 baking potatoes, about 2½ pounds	3 tablespoons grated cheese

Combine the Half & Half, bay leaf, and onion slices and simmer over low heat while preparing the potatoes. Peel and quarter the potatoes, then cut each quarter in half. Put them into a saucepan, cover with water, add some salt if desired, and cook for about 10 minutes. Drain. Strain Half & Half over potatoes, add nutmeg, pepper, and salt and simmer for another 5 minutes. Pour into a 1½-quart baking dish and refrigerate. Next day, sprinkle with cheese and reheat in a 350° F. oven, or at whatever temperature is being used for other dishes, for 30 minutes, less if the temperature is higher.

WARREN KINSMAN'S GINGERED CARROTS

3 pounds fresh carrots
6 tablespoons butter or margarine
6 teaspoons ground ginger

Scrape carrots and cut into ½-inch pieces. Cover with water and cook until very soft, about 45 minutes to an hour, depending upon age. Test by trying to mash them with a fork. Strain, return them to the saucepan, and toss over low heat to dry them well. Put the carrots in a food mill and purée. Melt the butter or margarine in a saucepan, but do not let it brown; add the ground ginger, mix, pour over carrots, and blend. Put the carrots into a bake-and-serve dish. Refrigerate and reheat the next day in a 350° F. oven for about 10 minutes.

FRESH MUSHROOMS AND WHITE WINE

3 pounds fresh mushrooms	1 tablespoon cornstarch
2 tablespoons butter or margarine	½ cup chopped parsley
½ cup white wine	

Wash mushrooms, trim off stems, slice larger ones, quarter small ones, and leave very small ones whole. Melt the butter or margarine in a large saucepan, add 2 tablespoons of the wine and all the mushrooms. Cover and simmer over low heat until mushrooms give up their juice. Stir occasionally and continue simmering until mushrooms are soft, about 20 minutes. Blend remaining wine with cornstarch and add to mushrooms. Stir and simmer until mushroom liquid is thickened. Cool and refrigerate. Next day, reheat and boil again. Just before serving, lower heat, add chopped parsley and do not allow to boil again.

BAKED STUFFED TOMATOES

6 large tomatoes	1½ tablespoons flour
1½ cups small elbow macaroni	1½ cups milk
Salted water	½ cup grated Cheddar cheese
1½ tablespoons butter	Salt and pepper to taste

Cut off tops of tomatoes and remove pulp. Reserve tops. Stand the tomatoes upside down to drain, then refrigerate. Cook the 1½ cups small elbow macaroni in salted water until soft, then drain. Put macaroni into a bowl. Melt the butter, add flour and blend; then add milk and cook, stirring constantly, until the sauce has thickened. Add cheese and stir until melted. Pour it over the macaroni and refrigerate. Next day, fill tomatoes with macaroni and cheese and put the tops back on. Preheat oven to 400° F., and bake the tomatoes for 20 minutes.

BOILED ONIONS IN CREAM SAUCE

2 pounds small white onions, fresh or canned (see Note)
¼ teaspoon nutmeg
3 tablespoons butter or margarine
3 tablespoons flour

1 cup milk
½ cup light cream or Half & Half
Salt and pepper to taste

Peel fresh onions, place them in a saucepan, and add enough water to cover well; add nutmeg and simmer for 35 minutes until tender. Refrigerate in the cooking water. Next day, drain the onions, melt the butter or margarine, add flour and blend. Stir in milk and cream or Half & Half and simmer until sauce is thickened; add onions and keep warm in a double boiler or water bath until ready to serve. Then reheat quickly.

N O T E :
For canned onions, drain all liquid from the onions and rinse with hot water, then add to the white sauce.

V A R I A T I O N :
For gratin onions, cut onions in half before boiling, drain, and place in a baking dish. Pour white sauce over the onions, sprinkle with dry

bread crumbs and grated cheese, and dot with butter. Bake for 15–20 minutes in a 350° F. oven.

SWEET AND SOUR BEANS AND CARROTS

3 cups fresh French-cut green
beans, or use one 10-ounce
package frozen French-cut
green beans
1½ cups sliced carrots, or use one
10-ounce package frozen
sliced carrots

3 tablespoons butter or margarine
2 tablespoons flour
2½ tablespoons sugar
2½ tablespoons wine vinegar or
lemon juice
Salt and pepper to taste

Cook green beans and carrots separately in boiling salted water, or follow individual package instructions; drain, but reserve cooking liquid. Melt the butter or margarine, add flour and blend. Add 1½ cups of the combined vegetable cooking liquids, stir to blend, and add sugar, vinegar or lemon juice, salt and pepper. Simmer for 5 minutes, then add the vegetables. Cool and refrigerate. Reheat the next day.

BAKED CABBAGE

5 cups white cabbage, chopped coarse
4 tablespoons butter or margarine
4 tablespoons flour
2 cups Half & Half
¼ teaspoon nutmeg

1 cup grated Cheddar cheese
Dry bread crumbs
Butter or margarine
Salt and pepper to taste

Cook chopped cabbage in enough salted water to cover for 2 minutes, then drain, shake dry, and set aside. Melt the butter or margarine, add flour and blend. Add Half & Half and nutmeg; stir well. Simmer the sauce for 5 minutes. Arrange one-third of the cabbage in a baking dish, sprinkle ⅓ cup cheese on top, cover with one-third of the white sauce. Sprinkle with bread crumbs, dot with butter or margarine, and white sauce, and finish with the remaining cabbage, cheese, and white sauce. Sprinkle with bread crumbs dot with butter or margarine, and refrigerate. Next day, preheat oven to 375° F., and bake for 30 minutes.

YELLOW TURNIPS AND MASHED POTATOES

2–2½ pounds yellow turnips   *½ cup Half & Half, hot*
5 baking potatoes, cubed   *Salt and pepper to taste*
½ stick butter or margarine, melted
(2 ounces)

Peel turnips and cut into ½-inch cubes, cover with water, add salt and cook for 16 minutes, until they just begin to get soft. Cool and refrigerate in the water. Peel potatoes and cut into ½-inch cubes, cover with water, add salt and cook for 15 minutes. Cool and refrigerate in the water.

Next day, reheat both turnips and potatoes and cook until very soft. Drain both well, shake dry, and press through a food mill or ricer. To the potatoes, add the melted butter and the hot Half & Half; blend well, then add mashed turnips and blend again. Set the pot with the mashed potato/turnip mixture into a larger pot to keep warm until needed. Reheat just before serving (see A Holiday Bird, page 160).

SWEET POTATO CASSEROLE

5–6 sweet potatoes, about 2 pounds   2 cups milk
Juice of 3 limes   ½ teaspoon salt
One 16-ounce can kernel corn, drained   ¼ teaspoon pepper
4 tablespoons butter or margarine   ¼ teaspoon nutmeg
4 tablespoons flour   Bread crumbs

Wash and peel potatoes, cut into cubes, cover with water and parboil for 5–6 minutes; drain, sprinkle with lime juice, and let stand for 10 minutes. Mix with drained corn, put into a baking dish, cool, and refrigerate.

Next day, preheat oven to 350° F. In a saucepan melt the butter or margarine, add flour and blend; to this mixture add milk, salt, pepper, and nutmeg and simmer for a few minutes. Pour over sweet potato/corn mixture, sprinkle with bread crumbs, and bake in the preheated oven for 45 minutes to an hour, until potatoes are tender.

RICE AND MUSHROOMS

1 cup converted rice   2 tablespoons chopped onion
2 cups chicken stock, homemade   1 pound mushrooms, washed and
    (see page 68) or canned   sliced
2 tablespoons butter or margarine   1 tablespoon soy sauce
2 tablespoons oil   ½ teaspoon pepper

Wash the rice and put it into a saucepan with a lid along with the chicken stock, and simmer, covered, until rice is almost done. Melt the butter or margarine, add oil, then onions and sauté until transparent. Next add mushrooms, soy sauce, and pepper. Stir until mushrooms give up some juice, then cover and cook for 10–15 minutes, until mushrooms are soft. When rice is almost done, put it into a baking dish along with the mushrooms and juice, mix, then cool and refrigerate. Next day, preheat oven to 350° F., cover baking dish, and bake for 20–25 minutes.

CORNMEAL GNOCCHIS

3 cups milk	*2 tablespoons butter*
3 cups yellow cornmeal	*1 cup grated Parmesan cheese*
1 teaspoon salt	*Butter*

In the top of a double boiler, directly on the flame, heat milk, add cornmeal and salt, and cook for 5 minutes, stirring constantly. Then place over boiling water and cook for another 30 minutes. Add butter and ½ cup of the cheese, and mix well. Butter a shallow roasting pan and spread the mixture out about 1 inch thick. Refrigerate.

Next day, preheat oven to 350° F. Cut the chilled cornmeal mixture into 1½-inch squares and arrange these squares in overlapping rows in a shallow baking dish. Sprinkle with the remaining ½ cup cheese and dot with butter. Bake in the preheated oven for 20–25 minutes. Serve instead of potatoes, or as a first course with tomato sauce.

EGGPLANT CASSEROLE

2 small eggplants	*½ cup grated Parmesan cheese*
1 cup light cream	*½ cup dry bread crumbs*
2 teaspoons soy sauce	*Butter*

Rinse, peel, and dice eggplants, put into a pot, cover with water and simmer until just tender, 15–20 minutes. Drain and put into a baking dish. Refrigerate. Next day, preheat oven to 375° F. Combine cream and soy sauce and pour over the eggplant. Combine cheese and bread crumbs and sprinkle over all. Dot with butter and bake for 20–30 minutes in the preheated oven.

HARVARD BEETS

3 cups canned beets, sliced, diced, or julienned
¾ tablespoon cornstarch
¾ cup sugar

½ cup beet juice
2 tablespoons vinegar
2 tablespoons lemon juice
3 tablespoons butter

Drain beets and reserve the juice. In a saucepan, combine cornstarch and sugar, add the beet juice, vinegar, and lemon juice and simmer until thickened. Add the beets, bring to the boiling point, then cool and refrigerate. Next day, reheat, add butter, stir to melt butter, and serve.

SALADS

HARLEQUIN COLESLAW

2 cups shredded white cabbage	*¼ cup grated green peppers*
1 cup shredded red cabbage	*Mayonnaise*
½ cup grated carrots	*½ cup grated Parmesan cheese*
½ cup grated radishes	

Combine all the vegetables, then add just enough mayonnaise to bind.
Finally, fold in the grated cheese. Refrigerate before serving.

RICE SALAD

1 cup brown rice	*6 bananas*
3 cups water	*2 teaspoons curry powder*
1 teaspoon salt	*¼ cup orange juice*

Wash rice, put it into a saucepan, add water and salt, and cook until rice is done. There should not be any water left. Put rice into a bowl and add 2 sliced bananas. Mash the remaining 4 bananas until they're liquefied. Add curry powder to the orange juice and simmer for 1 minute; then add to liquid bananas. Blend and pour the mixture over the rice and bananas. Cool and refrigerate.

ASPARAGUS SALAD

3–4 pounds fresh asparagus
Juice of 3 lemons
2 hard-cooked eggs, chopped
6 pimento strips

Cook asparagus according to directions for Fresh Asparagus (see page 174). Drain, place on a platter, and pour lemon juice over the hot asparagus. Baste with the juice while the asparagus are cooling. Next day, arrange on individual salad plates and sprinkle chopped eggs over the asparagus. Drape a pimento strip over each serving.

GREEN BEAN SALAD

Two 10-ounce packages frozen French-cut green beans
½ teaspoon dried summer savory
½ cup onion, chopped fine
¾ cup oil
3 tablespoons wine vinegar
1 teaspoon salt
½ teaspoon pepper
6 large lettuce leaves

Cook beans according to package instructions, but add summer savory; drain and shake well. Add onion and mix. Beat together until foamy the oil, vinegar, salt and pepper, and pour over hot beans. Mix, then cool and refrigerate. Next day, arrange the beans on lettuce leaves and serve as a salad.

VEGETABLE SALAD

One 10-ounce package frozen lima beans
One 10-ounce package frozen peas and carrots
One 10-ounce package frozen cauliflowerettes

Juice of 2 lemons
¾ cup mayonnaise
2 tablespoons grated onion
2 tablespoons chopped parsley

Cook vegetables separately according to individual package instructions. Drain and put them all into a bowl; sprinkle with lemon juice and toss. Mix mayonnaise with grated onion and parsley. Cool vegetables to room temperature then drain again. Add mayonnaise, mix, and refrigerate. Serve on salad plates instead of a vegetable.

BEANS AND MUSHROOM SALAD

1½ pounds fresh green beans, or use two 10-ounce packages frozen beans
½ pound fresh mushrooms
½ cup oil

3 tablespoons lemon juice
2 teaspoons prepared mustard
½ teaspoon salt
¼ teaspoon pepper

Wash and trim the fresh beans, cut them in half, drop them into boiling salted water, and cook at a rolling boil for 7 minutes; or cook frozen beans according to package instructions. Wash and slice the mushrooms, and cook in boiling salted water for 1 minute. Drain both vegetables and put into a bowl. Beat together until foamy the oil, lemon juice, mustard, salt, and pepper. Then pour the mixture over the still-warm vegetables. Stir to coat well. Refrigerate overnight.

SALAD OF PEAS AND CARROTS

Two 10-ounce packages frozen peas *⅛ teaspoon garlic salt*
  and carrots   *¼ teaspoon pepper*
2 tablespoons oil   *2 tablespoons grated onion*
½ tablespoon lemon juice   *2 tablespoons sour cream*

Cook peas and carrots according to package instructions. Drain and shake well to remove all moisture. Combine oil, lemon juice, garlic salt, pepper, and grated onion; beat until fluffy, then add to still-warm vegetables. Refrigerate. Next day, fold in the sour cream before serving.

ONION SALAD

1 pound yellow onions, preferably *½ tablespoon lemon juice*
  of uniform size   *½ teaspoon salt*
¾ cup water   *¼ teaspoon pepper*
¼ cup vinegar   *2 tablespoons sour cream or may-*
2 tablespoons oil   *onnaise*

Peel onions and slice rather thick; cut each slice in half. Combine water and vinegar and bring to the boiling point; add onions and boil for 30 seconds. Drain very well and put onions into a bowl. Combine oil, lemon juice, salt, and pepper and beat until foamy. Pour mixture over onions and mix to coat evenly. Refrigerate. Next day, fold in the sour cream or mayonnaise before serving.

JELLIED CUCUMBER SALAD WITH
GREEN SAUCE

4 large cucumbers	*1 teaspoon salt*
2 cups water	*1 package lime Jell-O*
½ cup wine vinegar	*1 envelope plain gelatin*
1 teaspoon sugar	

Peel cucumbers, cut them in half, and remove the seeds. Cut the halves in pieces, put them into a blender, add ½ cup of the water, and purée. In a saucepan combine the remaining 1½ cups of water with the vinegar, sugar, and salt. Sprinkle lime Jell-O powder and gelatin over the mixture and, while stirring constantly, slowly bring to just below the boiling point to dissolve the Jell-O and gelatin. Pour into a bowl, add cucumber purée, and taste for seasoning; then pour this mixture into a 1-quart mold or ring mold. Refrigerate until set or overnight, then unmold and serve with green sauce (see below).

THE GREEN SAUCE:

½ cup cottage cheese	*3 scallions, trimmed*
4 tablespoons plain yoghurt	*1 tablespoon prepared white*
4 sprigs parsley, trimmed of heavy	*horseradish, drained*
stems	*½ teaspoon dry mustard*
4 sprigs fresh dill, trimmed of	*1 teaspoon vinegar*
heavy stems	

Purée cottage cheese and yoghurt in a blender; gradually feed into the blender, with the motor running, the sprigs of parsley and dill. Wash and trim the scallions and feed them into the purée; finally add the horseradish, dry mustard, and vinegar.

ASPARAGUS MOUSSE

One 10-ounce package frozen
 asparagus
3 scallions, trimmed
½ cup cut-up celery
4 slices of onion
½ sliced carrot

1½ cups chicken stock, homemade
 (see page 68) or canned
2 envelopes plain gelatin
Salt and pepper to taste
1½ cups of heavy cream
6 large lettuce leaves

Cook asparagus according to package instructions and let cool. Trim scallions, slice, and put into the blender; add celery, onion, carrot, 1 cup of the chicken stock and purée. Cut 6 tips from the cooked asparagus and put them into individuals molds. Add the remaining asparagus to the blender and pureé again. Pour the purée into a bowl. In a saucepan, sprinkle gelatin over the remaining ½ cup of chicken stock and, while stirring constantly, heat to dissolve the gelatin. Add gelatin liquid to asparagus purée and stir. Taste for seasoning. Refrigerate until mixture begins to set. Whip cream until stiff, then fold into the asparagus purée. Divide among the 6 molds and refrigerate until completely set, or overnight. Unmold onto lettuce leaves and serve.

PART TWO

DESSERTS

PLAIN RHUBARB PUDDING

1 cup sugar
½ cup water
2 cups rhubarb, cut into 1-inch pieces and rinsed

In a saucepan with a tight-fitting lid, combine sugar and water, bring to the boiling point, and add the rhubarb; return to the boiling point and simmer for 1 minute. Do not stir, but shake pan. Remove from heat, cover tightly, and let stand for 1 hour. Then refrigerate. The rhubarb will remain in pieces.

RHUBARB TAPIOCA PUDDING

1 cup sugar
½ cup water
2 tablespoons Minute Tapioca
2 cups rhubarb, cut into 1-inch pieces and rinsed

Combine sugar and water and stir to dissolve sugar, then add Minute Tapioca; add rhubarb and, while stirring constantly, bring to the boiling point. Simmer for 2 minutes, again stirring constantly, until pudding is thickened. The rhubarb will be in shreds. Pour into a serving bowl and refrigerate.

GRAPEFRUIT MOUSSE

3 cups water
3 envelopes plain gelatin
1½ cups sugar
Two 6-ounce cans frozen unsweet-
ened grapefruit juice
½ cup orange-flavored
liqueur
1 cup heavy cream
Fresh strawberries, for
garnish (optional)

Put 2 cups of water into a 1½–2-quart saucepan. Sprinkle in the gelatin and add sugar. While stirring constantly, bring to just below the boiling point and make sure the gelatin and sugar have dissolved. Remove from heat, add the grapefruit juice, 1 cup water, and the orange-flavored liqueur. Stir mixture well to dissolve the grapefruit juice. Refrigerate until the mousse begins to set, then beat until fluffy. Beat heavy cream until stiff and fold into the fluffy grapefruit juice. Put into a serving bowl and refrigerate overnight. If desired, garnish with fresh strawberries.

STRAWBERRY MOUSSE

2 *pints fresh strawberries*	*1 cup white wine*
2 *cups water*	*1 cup heavy cream*
1 cup sugar	*½ cup sugar*
3 envelopes plain gelatin	*½ teaspoon vanilla extract*

Wash and hull the strawberries. Combine water and sugar and sprinkle with gelatin. While stirring constantly over low heat, bring mixture to just below the boiling point; then add wine. Put about ½ cup of this liquid into a blender, add berries and purée. Combine with remaining gelatin/sugar liquid and refrigerate until it begins to set. Beat strawberry gelatin until foamy; beat the heavy cream until stiff, gradually adding ½ cup sugar and the vanilla extract. Combine foamy strawberry purée and whipped cream. Pour into a serving bowl and refrigerate until set or overnight.

PEAR MOUSSE

4 pears	*¾ teaspoon ground ginger*
1 cup white wine	*2 envelopes plain gelatin*
1 cup water	*4 egg whites*
1 cup sugar	

Peel pears, core, and slice them. Combine pears, wine, water, sugar, and ginger. Bring to the boiling point, reduce heat, and simmer until pears are soft, depending upon the ripeness of the pears. Put ½ cup of the cooking liquid into a saucepan and chill a bit, then sprinkle with gelatin. Reheat, stirring constantly, to dissolve the gelatin. Put the pears, cooking liquid, and gelatin liquid into a blender and purée. Chill until almost set. Beat the pear purée, then beat the egg whites until stiff. First add some of the pear purée to the egg whites and fold in, then reverse and fold egg whites into pear purée. Pour into a serving bowl and refrigerate overnight.

CHERRIES OR BERRIES IN WHIPPED CREAM WITH GELATIN

Three 10-ounce packages frozen rasp-   *2 envelopes plain gelatin*
berries, or frozen cherries (ap-   *1 pint heavy cream*
proximately 2½ pounds in all)   *Sugar, as needed (see Note)*

Defrost fruits and collect the juice. To the juice add enough water to make 3 cups. Put the 3 cups of liquid into a saucepan, sprinkle with gelatin and, while stirring constantly over low heat, dissolve the gelatin. Put mixture into a bowl and refrigerate. When beginning to set, beat the gelatin mixture until fluffy. Beat the heavy cream until stiff, fold fluffy gelatin into whipped cream, then add the whole fruits. Pour into a serving bowl and refrigerate to set.

NOTE:
Addition of sugar, whether to the gelatin mixture or the whipped cream, depends upon the sweetness of the fruit selection.

GRAPES IN WINE ASPIC

¾ cup sugar   *2½ cups dry white wine*
¾ cup water   *1½ cups Thompson seedless grapes*
2 envelopes plain gelatin

Combine sugar and water, sprinkle gelatin on top and, while stirring constantly, slowly heat to just below the boiling point until the sugar and gelatin are dissolved. Cool to room temperature then add wine and refrigerate. (Do not add wine to hot sugar/gelatin mixture or the aspic may get cloudy.) Wash and stem the grapes. When aspic begins to set, add grapes and either divide among 6 individual dishes or pour into a serving bowl or mold. Refrigerate until set. If desired, serve with Sauce for Fruits (see page 118).

VARIATIONS:
Other fruits such as apples, fresh strawberries, or pears may be used instead of grapes.

MELON YOGHURT

1 cantaloupe	*2 tablespoons sugar*
2 envelopes plain gelatin	*¼ teaspoon vanilla extract*
½ cup water	*3 tablespoons grated almonds*
2 cups plain yoghurt	

Cut melon in half, remove seeds, then cut melon halves into strips. Cut strips crosswise into small pieces, then remove them by cutting close along the rind. Sprinkle gelatin over water in a small saucepan. Slowly bring to the boiling point, stirring constantly to dissolve gelatin. Cool to room temperature. Beat yoghurt with sugar and vanilla extract and add to the cooled gelatin. Mix well. Place a layer of melon pieces in the bottom of a serving dish, spoon some of the yoghurt/gelatin mixture over, then add more melon and more yoghurt until all is used. Refrigerate to set. Garnish with almonds grated in a Mouli grater.

VARIATION:
Mix the melon pieces with the yoghurt/gelatin mixture and divide among 6 individual dishes. Refrigerate to set and garnish with grated almonds.

MOCHA MOUSSE

3½ cups milk
2 ounces sweet chocolate
4 tablespoons sugar
2 tablespoons dry instant coffee

2 envelopes plain gelatin
1 cup heavy cream
1 tablespoon sugar
1 teaspoon vanilla extract

Combine 3 cups of the milk with the chocolate and sugar; simmer, stirring constantly, until chocolate and sugar are dissolved. Add instant coffee and heat to the boiling point until the coffee is dissolved. Sprinkle gelatin over the remaining ½ cup of milk and heat to the boiling point, stirring constantly, until the gelatin is dissolved. Add to the chocolate/coffee mixture. Cool and refrigerate. When beginning to set, beat until fluffy. Beat heavy cream until stiff, gradually adding sugar and vanilla extract. Combine jellied chocolate/coffee mixture with whipped cream and pour into a serving bowl. Refrigerate to set.

ORANGE FRUIT DESSERT

One 19-ounce can sliced peaches
One 10-ounce package frozen raspberries, defrosted
Two 10-ounce packages frozen strawberries, defrosted

2 envelopes plain gelatin
One 6-ounce can frozen orange juice

Drain peaches and reserve the liquid. Put peaches into a bowl and the drained-off liquid into a saucepan. Add the defrosted berries and their juice to the peaches. Sprinkle the gelatin over the drained-off peach liquid, stir, and gently heat to dissolve the gelatin, stirring constantly. Place still-frozen orange juice into a bowl and pour the dissolved gelatin mixture over it. Dissolve the orange juice, then chill to a heavy egg-white consistency. Beat, chill again, then beat until fluffy. Fold in the combined fruits (peaches and berries) with their juices, pour into a 7–8 cup serving bowl, and refrigerate until ready to serve.

FRUITS IN GRAPE JUICE ASPIC

5 small cans assorted fruits, such as sliced peaches, pears,
mandarin oranges, or pineapple chunks
2 envelopes plain gelatin
One 6-ounce can frozen grape juice

Drain fruits and reserve the juices. Measure juice and, if necessary, add enough water to make 2½ cups. Place the liquid in a saucepan, sprinkle gelatin on top, and heat slowly, stirring constantly to dissolve the gelatin. Place the still-frozen grape juice in a bowl and pour the gelatin liquid over it. Stir to dissolve grape juice. Chill to egg-white consistency. Add fruits and pour into a 6–8-cup serving bowl or into a fancy mold. Refrigerate until set. Serve directly from the serving bowl or unmold onto a platter.

If desired serve with the following sauce:

1 cup low fat cottage cheese
½ cup low fat yoghurt
3 tablespoons sugar
1 tablespoon grated nuts

Combine all the ingredients in a blender and process until very smooth.

NO-CRUST STRAWBERRY AND RHUBARB PIE

1 cup water
1 cup sugar
One 20-ounce bag frozen rhubarb,
defrosted
2 envelopes plain gelatin
One 16-ounce box frozen straw-
berries, defrosted

1 pint fresh strawberries
½ cup water
1 tablespoon sugar
1 teaspoon plain gelatin
2 teaspoons cornstarch

In a saucepan, combine water and sugar and bring to the boiling point. Add rhubarb, bring back to the boiling point, reduce heat, and simmer for about 3–4 minutes without stirring; then cover pan and remove from heat for 20 minutes. Pour off 1 cup of the accumulated liquid into a small saucepan, let cool a bit, then sprinkle with gelatin. Heat gently, stirring constantly to dissolve the gelatin. Add to the rhubarb, together with the defrosted strawberries. Stir, very gently, then pour into a 10-inch pie pan. Refrigerate until the mixture begins to set. Wash and hull the fresh strawberries, then set them upright in a ring around the edge of the pie. Arrange remaining berries in an attractive pattern in the center of the pie. Refrigerate. In a small saucepan, combine the ½ cup water with the tablespoon of sugar, the 1 teaspoon gelatin, and the 2 teaspoons cornstarch. Bring the mixture to the boiling point, over low heat, while stirring constantly. Spoon over the strawberry garnish and the rest of the pie to glaze it. Serve in wedges like any other pie, but run a knife around the edge first to loosen it. If desired, serve with Sauce for Fruits (see page 118).

OLD-FASHIONED BAKED RICE PUDDING

3 tablespoons uncooked regular rice   1 cup seedless raisins
Butter for pan   ¾ cup sugar
½ teaspoon salt   4 cups milk
¼ teaspoon nutmeg   Ground cinnamon, for garnish

Preheat oven to 325 ° F.

Wash rice and put it into a buttered 2-quart baking dish; add salt, nutmeg, raisins, and sugar. Pour the milk over all. Bake for 3 hours in the preheated oven. Stir about every half-hour to prevent the rice from settling at the bottom. Cool and refrigerate. Sprinkle with ground cinnamon before serving.

GINGERED PEARS

3 large pears   6 teaspoons ginger marmalade
2 cups water   2 envelopes plain gelatin
2 tablespoons sugar   2 cups ginger ale
½ teaspoon ground ginger

Peel the pears and very carefully cut them into halves. With a melon-ball cutter, remove core. Arrange in a saucepan and add water, sugar, and ginger and simmer until the pears begin to get soft. Let cool in the cooking liquid, then arrange in a serving bowl and reserve the liquid. Fill the cores with ginger marmalade, about 1 teaspoon each. Measure cooking liquid and add just enough water to make 2 cups. Sprinkle gelatin over it and, while stirring constantly, bring close to the boiling point to dissolve the gelatin. Cool and refrigerate. When beginning to set, add the ginger ale, mix, and pour over the pears in a serving dish. Refrigerate overnight.

CHEESE CAKE

This is Margaret O'Connor's mother's famous cheese cake. It was very popular in Highmount, New York, at the turn of the century.

Half a 4-ounce box of Zwieback
1½ cups sugar
5 tablespoons melted butter
1½ pounds cream cheese, at room temperature
6 large eggs, separated

1 large egg, whole
3 tablespoons flour
½ teaspoon salt
1 teaspoon lemon juice
1 teaspoon vanilla extract
1 pint sour cream

Preheat oven to 325° F.

Put the Zwieback into plastic bags and crush, either with a rolling pin (or by stepping on them). Do not use the blender; it makes the crumbs too fine. Combine crushed Zwieback with ½ cup of the sugar and the 5 tablespoons melted butter, and press the mixture into the bottom of a 9½-inch spring-form pan. Refrigerate. Put the softened cream cheese into a bowl. Beat the 6 egg whites until stiff. Using the same beater, beat the cream cheese, gradually adding 6 egg yolks, the whole egg, the remaining 1 cup of sugar, the flour, salt, lemon juice, vanilla extract, and finally the sour cream. When all is well mixed, fold one-third of the cream cheese mixture into the beaten egg whites. Then reverse the process, and fold the egg whites into the remaining cream cheese. There will be some lumps of egg white. Pour the cream cheese mixture into the prepared spring-form pan. Bake in the preheated oven for 1 hour and 15 minutes. Do not open the door, but let the cake stand in the turned-off oven for at least 1 more hour. Cool and refrigerate.

SAUCE FOR FRUITS

2 cups cottage cheese
1 cup plain yoghurt
4 tablespoons sugar
1 teaspoon vanilla extract

Combine all ingredients in a blender and purée until very smooth. Refrigerate before using. The sauce will thicken as it chills.

VARIATIONS:

Instead of sugar and vanilla extract, use 3 tablespoons honey and 2 tablespoons raisins, or use 3 tablespoons honey and 3 ounces of chopped nuts.

PART THREE

(ALL THE RECIPES ARE FOR EIGHT)

HORS D'OEUVRES
AND FIRST COURSES

MELON AND CANDIED GINGER

12 squares Persian or Cranshaw melon
12 small pieces candied ginger
12 toothpicks

Cut melon into ¾-inch squares and fasten a small piece of candied ginger to a melon square with a toothpick. Cover with plastic wrap and refrigerate for a few hours.

OPEN-FACED SANDWICHES

These can be made in the morning and served in the evening. They will not keep overnight.

OPEN-FACED CREAM CHEESE AND
SMOKED SALMON SANDWICHES

2 large, square slices of pumpernickel bread, or Kom-
missbrot
One 4-ounce package cream
cheese, at room tempera-
ture

¼ pound smoked salmon, sliced
thin
Fresh ground pepper

Spread bread with cream cheese, cover with smoked salmon, and press
down. Grate the pepper over the salmon and press again to make the
pepper stick. Cut each slice of bread into 6 squares. Cover with plastic
wrap and refrigerate for a few hours.

OPEN-FACED CREAM CHEESE AND
RADISH SANDWICHES

6 slices of Party Rye bread
Butter or cream cheese, at room temperature
Salt
Radishes

Spread bread with either butter or cream cheese and sprinkle with salt.
Wash, trim, and slice radishes. Arrange slices in neat overlapping
rows on the bread; do not salt radishes or they will weep. Press slices
down a bit, then cut each piece of bread in half. Cover with plastic
wrap and refrigerate for a few hours.

OPEN-FACED LIVERWURST AND
PICKLE SANDWICHES

6 slices of Party Rye bread
Butter, at room temperature
3 heavy slices of liverwurst, at room temperature
1 dill pickle

Spread bread with butter; cut liverwurst slices in half and spread half on each slice of bread. Peel the pickle, cut off 1 end, and with an apple corer remove the seeds. With a potato peeler cut off 12 thin slices. Cut bread slices in half, twist the thin pickle slices, and put 1 on each half; press down to make the pickle slice stick to the liverwurst. Cover with plastic wrap and refrigerate for a few hours.

OPEN-FACED LIVERWURST AND
ONION SANDWICHES

6 slices of Party Rye bread
Butter
6 thick slices of liverwurst
24 slivers of onion

Spread bread with butter, cut liverwurst slices in half, and spread half on each piece of bread. Then cut each slice of bread in half. With a potato peeler, cut thin slivers of onion. Arrange 2 slivers crosswise on each liverwurst sandwich and press down. Cover with plastic wrap and refrigerate for a few hours.

OPEN-FACED CREAM CHEESE, OLIVES, AND
NUTS SANDWICHES

4 ounces cream cheese, at room temperature
2 tablespoons chopped black olives
1 tablespoon nuts, chopped fine or grated
2 square slices of pumpernickel bread, or Kommissbrot

Combine cream cheese, olives, and nuts and mix well. Spread on bread slices and cut each slice into 6 squares. Cover with plastic wrap and refrigerate for a few hours.

OPEN-FACED CREAM CHEESE, ONION, AND
CAPERS SANDWICHES

4 ounces cream cheese, at room temperature
Salt to taste
1 tablespoon grated onion
2 square slices of pumpernickel bread, or Kommissbrot
2 tablespoons drained capers

Combine cream cheese, salt, and grated onion and spread over bread slices. Sprinkle each slice with 1 tablespoon drained capers, spreading them evenly and pressing down to make them stick to the cream cheese. Cut each slice into 6 pieces. Cover with plastic wrap and refrigerate for a few hours.

OPEN-FACED STRIPED HAM AND
CHEESE SANDWICHES

2 slices of pumpernickel bread, or Kommissbrot
Butter
4 square slices of ham
4 square slices of cheese (American, Swiss, or Muenster)

Spread bread with butter and put a slice of ham on each. Top with a slice of cheese but let a strip of ham show at 1 edge. Cut the other 2 slices of ham in half and put them on top of the cheese slices, this time letting a strip of cheese show. Finally cut the remaining cheese slices in half and put on top of the ham slice, with a strip of ham showing. Trim off any overlap. Cut each slice of bread into 6 pieces. Cover with plastic wrap and refrigerate for a few hours.

BLUE CHEESE BITES

2 ounces blue cheese, at room
temperature
1 tablespoon whiskey
1/4 stick butter (1 ounce)
4 slices of thin white bread (kind
used for Melba toast)

2 slices of dark pumpernickel
bread
1 jar pimento cheese spread
Butter, at room temperature

Mash together the blue cheese and whiskey, and blend in the butter. Spread half the blue cheese on 1 slice of the white bread and top with 1 slice of pumpernickel. Butter the slice of pumpernickel and then spread with half the pimento cheese spread; butter a second slice of white bread and put it, buttered side down, on the pimento cheese spread. Wrap in waxed paper and chill. Repeat with remaining 2 slices of white bread and 1 slice of pumpernickel. Just before serving, cut each package of bread into 6 squares or 6 triangles.

EGG TIDBITS

3 hard-cooked eggs
1/2 stick butter, at room temperature (2 ounces)
1 teaspoon anchovy paste

12 Melba toast crackers
Butter, as needed
12 slices of stuffed green olive

Peel and slice the eggs; select 12 whole slices. Blend butter and an-chovy paste, and spread on crackers. Put an egg slice on top of each cracker, then top with a tiny dab of butter and a slice of olive. The butter will glue the olive to the egg slice. Refrigerate before serving.

PARSLEY-STUFFED EGGS

6 *hard-cooked eggs*	*⅛ teaspoon dry mustard*
1 tablespoon chopped parsley	*Salt and pepper to taste*
½ teaspoon grated onion	*Mayonnaise*

Cut the eggs in half crosswise through the middle. Carefully remove yolks and cut a small piece off the bottom of the egg cups to make them stand straight. Rub egg yolks through a sieve; add to the yolks, parsley, grated onion, dry mustard, salt and pepper, and just enough mayonnaise to bind—it does not take much. Refill the egg-white cups and refrigerate before serving.

CHICKEN LIVER PIE

½–¾ pound chicken livers	*1 teaspoon salt*
1 cup light cream	*½ teaspoon pepper*
4 eggs	*Butter for pan*
1 teaspoon dried tarragon	

Preheat oven to 325° F.

Drain livers and put them into a blender along with ½ cup of the cream, and purée. Put the eggs into a bowl, beat lightly, and add the remaining ½ cup of cream; beat again, then add tarragon, salt, and pepper. Finally, blend in the puréed chicken livers. Butter a 10-inch pie pan very well and pour in the chicken liver mixture. Bake in the preheated oven (not higher) for 30–40 minutes, until center of pie is set.

THIS WILL SERVE UP TO 10 AS A FIRST COURSE.

SCALLOPS AND MUSHROOMS

¾–1 pound scallops	*¾ cup white wine or dry ver-*
3 tablespoons butter or margarine	*mouth*
¾ pound mushrooms, chopped	*1½ teaspoons cornstarch*
3 teaspoons soy sauce	*8 slices of white toast*

Rinse scallops and pick them over for shell pieces; cut the small ones in half and quarter the larger ones. Melt the butter or margarine in a saucepan with a lid; add chopped mushrooms and soy sauce. Over low heat, cook mushrooms until they begin to give out some juice; cover and cook for about 15 minutes longer. Add scallops and cook for 5 minutes; blend wine and cornstarch and add to the mixture. Simmer until the sauce has thickened. Cut toast into points and arrange on 8 small serving dishes. Divide the mushroom/scallop mixture among them and serve.

BELGIAN ENDIVES WRAPPED IN
HAM AND CHEESE

8 large Belgian endives	*1 teaspoon salt*
1 cup milk	*8 slices of boiled ham*
1 cup water	*8 slices of Swiss cheese*

Preheat oven to 375° F.–400° F.

Trim endives and put them into a saucepan that holds them easily; add milk, water, and salt. Bring to the boiling point, then lower heat and simmer for 20 minutes. Drain off liquid, remove endives, and hold them upside down with tongs to drain all liquid. Wrap each endive first in a slice of ham then in a slice of cheese, and arrange in a baking dish in a single layer. Put the endives into the preheated oven and bake until cheese begins to melt. Serve directly from the baking dish.

FANCY FIRST COURSE PLATTERS

Jean Thackrey does these with a lot of imagination and whimsy; variety is the secret. Select from the following lists, allowing 8–10 items per person. Do not line the plate with lettuce. An 8-inch plate is about right.

FISH	VEGETABLES	OTHER
1 sardine	1 pickled mushroom	A wedge of hard-cooked egg
1–2 anchovies	A wedge of tomato	
1 smoked oyster	A teaspoon of cole-	½ slice of salami
A piece of smoked salmon	slaw	A piece of pastrami
	2 cucumber slices	A piece of liver paté
A piece of pickled herring	1 gherkin	
	1 cherry tomato	
A teaspoon of small shrimp with a bit of mayonnaise	1 scallion	
	1 pickled artichoke	
	1 or 2 olives	
A piece of sturgeon	1 or 2 dilled green beans	
	1 sprig of watercress	

SOUPS

GREEN PEA SOUP

Two 10-ounce packages frozen green peas

3½ cups chicken stock, homemade (see page 68) or canned

1 tablespoon soy sauce

½ cup light cream

Grated almonds or croutons

Put frozen peas into a saucepan, add the chicken stock and soy sauce, and cook until the peas are very soft. Put the mixture into a blender and purée; add the cream and pour back into the saucepan. Reheat and serve in cups, with grated almonds or croutons.

CREAM OF SPINACH SOUP

This is a hot version of Jean Thackrey's famous spinach soup.

One 10-ounce package frozen spinach
1/4 teaspoon nutmeg
1/4 cup chopped onion
3 tablespoons butter

2 cups chicken stock, homemade (see page 68) or canned
2 cups milk
Salt and pepper to taste
Sour cream and paprika (optional)

Cook spinach according to package instructions, but add nutmeg. Sauté the onions in butter until transparent, but do not brown. Combine spinach, onion, and chicken stock in a blender and purée; add to milk and heat to the boiling point. Taste for seasoning. If desired, top each serving with a spoonful of sour cream and dust with paprika.

TOMATO AND RICE SOUP

5 cups chicken stock, homemade (see page 68) or canned
One 16-ounce can peeled tomatoes
1 large onion, chopped, about 3/4 cup

1/2 teaspoon dried basil
1/2 teaspoon oregano
5 tablespoons Minute Rice
Chopped parsley, for garnish

In a saucepan, combine all ingredients except the rice and the parsley; simmer for a half-hour, then purée mixture in a blender. Return to saucepan, reheat to the boiling point, then add the rice. Let boil for a second or so, then turn off the heat and let stand for 5 minutes. Serve garnished with chopped parsley.

ONION SOUP

4 large onions
6 tablespoons butter or margarine
1 tablespoon olive oil
1 teaspoon sugar
4 cups beef stock, homemade (see page 69) or canned

3 cups chicken stock, homemade (see page 68) or canned
Parmesan cheese
8 slices of French bread

Slice onions very thin, melt the butter or margarine, add oil, and sauté onions until they begin to brown; then sprinkle with sugar and heat until sugar becomes dark brown. Add beef and chicken stock, and simmer for 30–45 minutes, until onions are soft. Toast the French bread, put a slice in each soup bowl, and add the onion soup. Serve Parmesan cheese on the side.

VARIATIONS:
Use 6 cups of beef stock and 1 cup of red wine or port wine; or use 6 cups of chicken stock and 1 cup of white wine; or use all beef stock or all chicken stock.

Or, ladle soup into ovenproof dishes and top each serving with toast and grated Swiss cheese; bake until the cheese is melted. Or, ladle soup into ovenproof dishes, spread toast with Roquefort cheese spread, and put it on top of the onion soup; bake until cheese bubbles. A 350° F. oven should be sufficient.

CORN SOUP

12 ears fresh corn
6 cups water
½ stick butter or margarine (2 ounces)

2 tablespoons flour
2 cups milk
Salt and pepper to taste

Grate corn off the cob and reserve. Cover the cobs with water and simmer for 30 minutes. Melt the butter or margarine, add flour and blend; then add the milk and stir to dissolve. Drain liquid off the cobs, discard cobs, and add liquid to the butter/flour/milk mixture; then add grated corn and simmer for 15–20 minutes, until corn is cooked. Season with salt and pepper to taste.

AVGOLEMONO SOUP

This is a famous soup—a very delicate soup—and the secret is steady beating while mixing. It can be made ahead of time and kept warm in a double boiler over hot but not boiling water.

¾ cup uncooked rice
7 cups chicken stock, homemade (see page 68) or canned
4 eggs, separated
Juice of 2 lemons

Wash rice, put it into a saucepan, cover with 5 cups of the chicken stock, and cook for 20–25 minutes, until the rice is done. Set aside. Beat the egg whites until stiff, add the egg yolk 1 at a time, and continue beating; add lemon juice, drop by drop, beating constantly (do not add lemon juice all at once). Heat the remaining 2 cups of chicken stock to just below the boiling point and, very slowly, add the stock to the beaten eggs, remembering to beat constantly. Finally combine the eggs and rice soup and keep warm over hot but not boiling water.

ODDS AND ENDS CHICKEN SOUP

½ chicken breast, skinned and
    boned
Juice of ½ lemon
¼ teaspoon ground ginger
2 cups leftover vegetables, such
    as peas, carrots, green

beans, cauliflower,
    Brussels sprouts
½ cup orzo
7 cups chicken stock, homemade
    (see page 68) or
    canned

Cut the raw chicken breast into strips, put into a bowl, sprinkle with lemon juice, and dust with ginger. Rinse off sauce from any creamed vegetable. Combine orzo and chicken stock in a pot and simmer for 15 minutes, until orzo is cooked. Add vegetables and chicken strips to the orzo and cook for another 5–10 minutes, then serve.

VARIATION:
If available, add ¾–1 cup cooked chicken or turkey instead of raw chicken strips.

CHICKEN SOUP WITH ANCHOVY CUSTARD

6 anchovy fillets
1 cup light cream
2 eggs

Butter for pan
7 cups chicken stock, homemade (see page 68)
    or canned

Preheat oven to 325° F.

Drain anchovies and put them into a blender, add cream, and purée. Beat eggs and add the anchovy/cream mixture. Butter an 8-inch pie pan and pour the custard mix into it. Bake in the preheated oven for 30–40 minutes until center is set. It is done when a knife inserted in the center comes out clean. Refrigerate. When ready to serve, cut custard into 8 wedges. Put 1 wedge in each of 8 soup bowls, heat chicken stock to the boiling point, and pour over.

NOTE:

For a first course, double the custard recipe and proceed as above; serve with sliced tomatoes and watercress.

WATERCRESS SOUP

1 bunch watercress
5 cups beef stock, homemade (see page
69) or canned, or use vegetable
stock (see page 69)
¼ teaspoon nutmeg

2 slices of onion
3 tablespoons butter
2 tablespoons flour
2 cups milk
Salt and pepper to taste

Cut up watercress and add to 3 cups of the beef stock; add nutmeg and onion, bring to the boiling point and simmer for 5 minutes. Put the mixture into a blender and purée. Pour it into a saucepan and add the remaining 2 cups of stock. In another saucepan, melt the butter, blend in the flour and add milk; stir well, then slowly bring mixture to the boiling point. Simmer for 5 minutes, then add puréed watercress liquid. Taste for seasoning and simmer for 10 minutes more before serving.

CHEESE SOUP

4 tablespoons butter
¾ cup chopped onion
1 cup grated carrots
3 tablespoons flour
6 cups chicken stock, homemade
(see page 68) or
canned

1 cup Half & Half
8 ounces grated Cheddar cheese
Salt and pepper to taste
Croutons

Melt butter, add onions, and sauté until the onions begin to get soft; add the grated carrots and sauté for a few minutes longer. Sprinkle with flour, blend in, then add stock and simmer for 20 minutes. Add Half & Half and cheese and keep the mixture below the simmering point until the cheese is melted, stirring most of the time. Taste for seasoning and serve with croutons.

ASPARAGUS SOUP

Cooking water and ends from asparagus   *5 tablespoons butter*
  (see Fresh Asparagus, page 174),   *5 tablespoons flour*
      about 4 cups liquid   *1½ cups Half & Half*
8 asparagus stalks, either fresh or leftover   *Salt and pepper to taste*

Put the ends and some of the water into a blender and purée in easy stages. Heat until warm, then strain through a fine sieve to remove the fibrous matter. If fresh asparagus is used, cut the spears into ¾-inch pieces and cook in some of the asparagus cooking water until soft. Strain the cooking water into the strained purée. Or cut leftover asparagus into ¾-inch pieces and reserve for garnish. Melt the butter, add flour and blend; add Half & Half and stir until smooth. The whole is then added to the asparagus purée and seasoned with salt and pepper to taste. Bring to the boiling point. Divide the asparagus pieces among 8 serving cups and ladle the soup over them.

FISH

HADDOCK IN CIDER OR APPLE JUICE

3–4 pounds haddock, tail end preferred
Butter for baking dish
Salt and pepper
1 lemon
1 tablespoon oil or margarine

1 onion, chopped fine
1 clove garlic, crushed
1 cup cider or apple juice
2 tomatoes, peeled and sliced
1 tablespoon chopped parsley

Preheat oven to 350° F.

Rinse fish and trim off fins or other bones. Select a baking dish large enough to hold the fish. Butter it well, sprinkle the fish with salt and pepper and the juice of ½ lemon. Slice the remaining ½ lemon and arrange on top of fish. Heat oil or margarine and sauté the chopped onion for about 5 minutes; add the garlic and the cider or apple juice, and pour over fish. Arrange tomato slices on top and around the fish.

Sprinkle with chopped parsley and bake in the preheated oven for 30–45 minutes, depending upon thickness. Serve directly from the baking dish.

STUFFED BASS

One whole 4–5 pound bass
Lemon juice
2 cups bread cubes, made from white
    bread with the crusts removed
Clam juice

2 tablespoons drained capers
½ stick butter or margarine,
    melted (2 ounces)
Additional melted butter for
    brushing fish

Preheat oven to 425° F.

Wash fish and rub the inside with lemon juice. Toast the bread cubes in the oven until lightly browned, then put them into a bowl. Add enough clam juice to moisten, then add capers, melted butter, and blend. Stuff the fish cavity with the bread mixture, stick 4–5 small skewers through the belly skin on both sides, and lace around the skewers with kitchen string. Line a roasting pan with cheesecloth, leaving enough overlap to fold over fish. Brush fish on one side with butter, then put the buttered side down on cheesecloth; brush the other side with butter and fold cheesecloth over. Bake in the preheated oven for 40 minutes if the fish weighed 4 pounds, for 45 minutes if it weighed 5 pounds. A rule of thumb is 10 minutes per pound up to 4 pounds, then 5 minutes more for each additional pound. Lift the fish out in the cheesecloth and turn onto a serving platter.

POACHED SALMON

One whole 5–6 pound salmon	*1 carrot*
1 or 2 lemons	*1 onion*
10 cups water	*1 bay leaf*
A few fresh dill stems	*4 tablespoons salt*
A few sprigs parsley	*3 cups white wine*
3 ribs of celery with tops	

Measure the thickness of the salmon.

Wash fish inside and out and rub the inside with lemon. Combine water, dill, parsley, celery, carrot, onion, bay leaf, and salt in a large pot and simmer for an hour and a half. Strain the liquid. Line a roasting pan with a double thickness of cheesecloth, allowing quite a bit to hang over the sides. Place the salmon on top, pour the white wine over it, and then add enough of the strained vegetable broth to cover completely. Place the roasting pan over 2 burners and bring liquid to the boiling point; then reduce heat and simmer. If the salmon is 3 inches thick at the thickest part, the cooking time will be 30 minutes; if thicker, allow more time. Poaching time is 10 minutes to the inch. To test fish for doneness, scrape off a small piece of the skin and lift the meat at the backbone.

When done, use potholders to grasp the overlapping cheesecloth and lift the fish out onto a serving platter. Remove skin from the topside and wipe off any accumulated water with paper towels. Turn the platter so that the belly side is nearest you, then, with the aid of the cheesecloth, turn the fish, using the heavier backside as a pivot. Remove the cheesecloth, scrape off the skin from the other side, and clean the platter. Serve immediately with horseradish cream sauce (see below).

HORSERADISH CREAM SAUCE:

1 cup heavy cream
4 ounces hot prepared white horseradish, drained and pressed dry
½ teaspoon salt

Whip the cream and combine it with horseradish and salt.

POACHED CODFISH

5–6 pounds codfish, in 1 piece	*5 tablespoons butter*
Juice of 1 lemon	*4 tablespoons flour*
6 cups water	*1½ cups Half & Half*
1 onion	*¾ cup fish cooking liquid*
1 bay leaf	*Salt and pepper to taste*
2 teaspoons salt	*4 hard-cooked eggs, chopped*
½ cup dill stems	

Wash codfish, rub with lemon juice, and measure the thickness of the fish. Combine water, onion, bay leaf, salt, and dill stems and simmer for 30–40 minutes. Wrap cheesecloth around the fish allowing for a generous overlap. Place into a large saucepan and strain the broth over the fish. Poach 10 minutes, for each inch of thickness. Melt the butter, add flour and blend. Stir in Half & Half until smooth.

With the help of the cheesecloth, remove the cooked fish to a serving platter and scrape off the top skin. Again with the help of the cheese-cloth, turn the fish and remove the skin from the other side. Clean the serving platter with paper towels and keep warm while finishing sauce. Measure ¾ cup of fish cooking liquid, add it to the cream sauce, and taste for seasoning. Bring sauce to the boiling point and simmer until thickened. If need be, dilute with more fish cooking liquid. Add chopped eggs and serve egg sauce on the side.

SHRIMP FRICASSEE

2½ pounds peeled frozen shrimp,   4 tablespoons butter
     small or medium sized   4 tablespoons flour
6 cups water   1 cup white wine
1 teaspoon salt   1 pound mushrooms
1 onion   One 10-ounce package frozen arti-
1 bay leaf   choke hearts
1 bunch fresh dill

Keep shrimp frozen until ready to use. To make cooking stock, put water, salt, onion, and bay leaf into a pot. Wash the dill and trim off heavy stems. Add the stems to the water; chop and reserve the leaves. Bring water to the boiling point and simmer for 30–40 minutes. Melt the butter, add flour and blend. Add ½ cup of the wine and set aside.

Wash and slice mushrooms, put them into a saucepan, and add the remaining ½ cup of wine. Simmer for 15 minutes and set aside. Cook the artichoke hearts according to package instructions; when done, drain and cool, then cut each in half. When the cooking stock is ready, put the frozen shrimp into a saucepan and strain the cooking liquid over. Bring to the boiling point over high heat, but watch it because it tends to foam. As soon as the liquid has come to a rolling boil, drain the shrimp and reserve 1 cup of cooking liquid. Add this to the butter/flour/wine mixture. Stir until smooth and cook until thickened; then add the mushrooms and wine, the shrimp, and the artichoke hearts. Keep below the boiling point so shrimp do not get tough. If the sauce is too heavy, add more wine. Add the chopped dill leaves at the last minute and serve over rice, with green peas or asparagus.

BAKED WHOLE FLOUNDER

8 flounder, about 1 pound each
Lemon juice
8 slices of bacon

Preheat oven to 400° F.

Cut off heads of fish and clean. Trim tails and fins, and rinse fish in
salted water and pat dry. With a sharp knife, make 2 gashes in the
dark topside skin, but try not to cut into the flesh underneath. Rub
the fish with lemon juice, put a slice of bacon on the gashed side of
each one, and arrange, slightly overlapping, on a rimmed cookie sheet.
Bake for 15 minutes in the preheated oven. Even if fish is less than 1
inch thick, this will allow for the fact that the skin is thick and the
flesh is not directly exposed to the heat.

BAKED SEA TROUT

5 pounds small sea trout, approximately   *Butter or margarine*
           4 fish   *8 ounces sour cream*
2 lemons   *3 tablespoons drained capers*
2 bunches parsley

Preheat oven to 425° F.

Measure fish at its thickest point and allow 10 minutes per inch baking time. Clean fish and split. Rub all over with lemon and squeeze
some lemon juice over each half. Put some parsley sprigs on one half
of each fish, dot with butter or margarine, and put the other half of
the fish back on top. Arrange the fish on an oiled baking sheet, top
with more butter, and bake for the calculated time. When fish is done,
remove and discard the parsley sprigs. Blend sour cream with drained
capers and serve on the side.

BAKED BLUEFISH

4–5 pounds bluefish, 1 or more fish
Sliced lemons
Melted butter or margarine
1 cup of white wine

Preheat oven to 425° F.

Measure fish at its thickest point and allow 10 minutes baking time for each inch of thickness. Clean fish well and rinse with salted water. Put a few slices of lemon in the cavity. Line a baking pan with lemon slices and put fish on top; brush with melted butter and add about 1 cup white wine. Bake in the preheated oven for the calculated time. Serve directly from the baking pan.

BAKED MACKEREL

4–5 pounds mackerel, or kingfish
Lemon juice
Butter or margarine
4 tomatoes

Preheat oven to 425° F.

Measure fish at its thickest point and allow 10 minutes baking time per inch. Clean fish and rub inside and out with lemon juice. Butter a baking dish and put the fish in it. Dot fish with butter or margarine. Cut the tomatoes in half and arrange around fish. Bake in the preheated oven for the calculated time, and serve directly from the baking dish.

BAKED HALIBUT

4 pounds halibut filet	4 tablespoons chopped onion
1 cup white wine	6 tablespoons butter
1 cup water	1 teaspoon salt
3/4 cup sliced onions	3 tablespoons flour
6 sprigs parsley	2 teaspoons lemon juice
1 bay leaf	1/4 teaspoon paprika
8 peppercorns	1/2 cup heavy cream
8 strips of bacon	

Preheat oven to 375° F.

Rinse the filets and measure the thickest point; allow 12 minutes baking time for each inch of thickness. Cut filets into 8 serving pieces and set aside. Combine wine, water, sliced onion, parsley, bay leaf, and peppercorns in a saucepan and simmer for 20 minutes. In a skillet, fry the bacon until limp and just beginning to get brown. Put bacon strips on paper towels to drain. Pour off all but 2 tablespoons of fat, add chopped onion and sauté until transparent. Use 3 tablespoons of the butter to grease a baking dish large enough to hold the fish in a single layer. Put fish filets close together in the dish and sprinkle with salt. Divide the sautéed onions among the fish filets and top each one with a strip of bacon. Strain the wine broth over the fish and bake in the preheated oven for the calculated time. Discard bacon. Strain the baking liquid into a bowl and keep fish warm. Melt the remaining 3 tablespoons butter, add flour and blend; add 1 1/2 cups of the reserved cooking liquid and stir. Simmer until sauce is thickened, then add lemon juice and paprika. Whip heavy cream until stiff and blend into the sauce. Top each filet with some of the sauce and serve the rest on the side.

BAKED FILET OF HADDOCK

3–3½ pounds filet of haddock
Juice of 2 lemons
½ teaspoon salt
¼ teaspoon pepper
1 large onion, sliced
1½ cups white wine

1 bay leaf
¼ teaspoon dried marjoram
3 tablespoons butter or margarine
2 tablespoons flour
½ cup light cream

Preheat oven to 400° F.

Rinse fish and wipe dry; measure the thickest point and allow 10–12 minutes per inch baking time. Mix lemon juice with salt and pepper and pour over the fish filets. Select a baking dish large enough to hold fish pieces in a single layer. Arrange onion slices at the bottom and put fish pieces on top. Combine white wine, bay leaf, and marjoram and bring to the boiling point. Pour this mixture over the fish and bake in the preheated oven for the calculated time. Drain and reserve liquid from the baking dish, but leave fish pieces in the dish. Knead butter or margarine with flour and add to fish cooking liquid. Cook over low heat until thickened, then add cream. Return just to the boiling point and pour over fish. Serve directly from the baking dish.

BAKED SMELTS

4 pounds smelts
¾ cup light cream
8 tablespoons flour
1½ teaspoons salt
1 teaspoon pepper

Approximately ¾ cup cooking oil
3 tablespoons butter or margarine
2 cups clam juice
2 teaspoons anchovy paste
3 tablespoons chopped parsley
2 teaspoons lemon juice
4 tablespoons grated Parmesan cheese

Preheat oven to 400° F.

Clean fish, cut off heads and tails, wash in salted water, and dry. Put cream into a bowl. Combine 5 tablespoons of the flour with the salt and pepper and put onto a plate. Dip the smelts in cream and roll in the seasoned flour. Heat oil over low heat and sauté fish for 7–8 minutes, until browned. Arrange fish in a baking dish. Combine the 3 tablespoons butter or margarine with the remaining 3 tablespoons of flour and blend. Add clam juice, blending well, and heat until smooth and thickened; then season with anchovy paste, parsley, and lemon juice. Pour the sauce over the smelts and sprinkle with cheese. When ready to serve, bake fish in the preheated oven for 10 minutes, until cheese begins to brown. Serve directly from the baking dish.

MACKEREL FILETS IN A SPICY SAUCE

8 filets of mackerel	*6 sprigs parsley*
Juice of 1 lemon	*1 teaspoon salt*
1 onion, sliced	*1½ cups water*
1 rib of celery, chopped	*¾ cup white wine*
3 whole cloves garlic	*3 tablespoons butter or margarine*
3 whole peppercorns	*3 tablespoons flour*
½ carrot, sliced	

Preheat oven to 400° F.

Rinse fish, pat dry, put into a bowl, and pour lemon juice over it. Let stand. Combine onion, celery, garlic, peppercorns, carrot, parsley, salt, and water in a saucepan and simmer for 30 minutes. Arrange fish filets in a baking dish in a single layer, skin side down; strain the seasoned broth over the filets, add the wine, and bake in the preheated oven for 15 minutes. Melt the butter or margarine, add flour and blend. When fish filets are done, pour off 1½ cups of the baking liquid and add it to the butter/flour blend. Stir to dissolve and cook until thickened. Taste for seasoning. Put fish onto a serving platter, spoon some of the sauce over it, and serve the rest of the sauce on the side.

FISH PUDDING

2 pounds fish filets (either scrod,   *3 tablespoons flour*
     halibut, or flounder)   *¾ cup milk*
Salt   *¼ cup clam juice*
1 lemon, cut in half   *4 ounces grated Parmesan cheese*
Butter for baking dish   *3 eggs, separated*
3 tablespoons butter or margarine

Preheat oven to 325° F.

Rinse filets, pat dry, sprinkle lightly with salt, and rub with lemon. Cut into small cubes and set aside. Butter a 2-quart baking dish very well. Melt 3 tablespoons butter or margarine, add flour and blend; add milk and clam juice and cook until sauce thickens. Add cheese and then, 1 after the other, the egg yolks. Add the fish. Beat egg whites until stiff and fold into fish mixture. Pour into prepared baking dish, and bake in the preheated oven for 1–1½ hours, until center is set and top is browned. Serve with rice and green peas.

POACHED RED SNAPPER

THE FISH:

     5–6 pounds red snapper
     2 lemons
     Water to cover
     1 tablespoon salt

THE SAUCE:

5 tablespoons butter or margarine	¾ cup poaching liquid
4 tablespoons flour	½ teaspoon dry mustard
1½ cups milk	½ cup chopped dill

Measure fish at the thickest point; poaching time is 10 minutes per inch of thickness. Clean fish and rub all over with lemon, inside and out. Reserve lemons. Line a pot large enough to hold the fish, with cheesecloth, allowing a generous overlap. Fill with enough water to cover fish and add salt; bring to the boiling point, then add fish and reserved lemons. Poach for the calculated time: begin timing at the moment the water boils again.

Prepare the sauce: Melt butter or margarine, blend in flour, and add milk and poaching liquid. Add mustard and simmer until thickened. Cook for 5 minutes, then add dill and remove from heat.

MEAT AND POULTRY

VEAL STEW WITH ARTICHOKES AND DILL SAUCE

3–4 pounds stewing veal

Two 10¾-ounce cans chicken broth

2 cups white wine

4 shallots or green onions

Two 10-ounce packages frozen artichoke hearts

2 tablespoons cornstarch

2 tablespoons chopped fresh dill

Combine veal, chicken broth, wine, and shallots or onions and simmer until veal is fork tender, about 1 hour. Add frozen artichoke hearts, and cook for 10 minutes more until the artichokes are barely done. Blend the 2 tablespoons cornstarch with a little water and gradually add to the stew to slightly thicken sauce. Simmer for 3 minutes. Turn off the heat and add the chopped dill; do not reheat. Serve immediately, with rice.

SMOTHERED PORK SHOULDER

3 ½ pounds boned pork shoulder,   *½ teaspoon pepper*
     also known as pork blade   *1 teaspoon caraway seeds*
4 cups chopped onion, about 3 large   *½ cup water*
1 teaspoon salt

Preheat oven to 375° F.

Rinse pork and pat dry. Place in a lidded casserole that is just large enough to hold the roast. Pack chopped onions around and over the roast, sprinkle with salt, pepper, and caraway seeds, add water, and cover. Roast, covered, for 2 hours, then uncover and continue cooking until the internal temperature of the meat reaches 185°, approximately 30–45 minutes longer. Remove meat from casserole and keep warm. Put remaining contents into a saucepan, skim off as much fat as possible, reheat, and serve as gravy.

MEAT LOAF

2½–3 pounds ground chuck   *½ teaspoon pepper*
6 slices of white bread   *1 teaspoon dried marjoram*
1 tablespoon steak sauce   *1 grated onion*
2 tablespoons ketchup   *3 eggs*
1 teaspoon salt   *1 sliced onion*

Preheat oven to 325° F.

Bring meat to room temperature and put into a bowl. Moisten bread with water and when soft, drain and squeeze dry. Add softened bread, steak sauce, ketchup, salt, pepper, marjoram, grated onion, and eggs to meat. Blend all together with both hands, squeezing it through your fingers. Put the sliced onion into a roasting pan. Shape meat into a loaf on top of the onions; this will prevent meat loaf from sticking to the pan. With wet hands, smooth surface of meat loaf. Roast for 1–1½ hours in the preheated oven. Let stand for a half-hour before slicing.

SAUERBRATEN

4–5 pounds bottom round roast

THE MARINADE:

¾ cup red wine	*1 teaspoon whole peppercorns*
¾ cup vinegar	*1 teaspoon juniper berries*
3 cups water	*1 sliced onion*
2 bay leaves	

TO POT ROAST:

¾ cup chopped onion
¾ cup chopped carrots
½ cup chopped celery leaves
3 cups marinade

THE SAUCE:

⅔ cup ginger snaps, crumbled
Reserved marinade

Put meat into a deep stainless steel, glass, or pottery bowl. In a saucepan, combine wine, vinegar, water, bay leaves, peppercorns, juniper berries, and sliced onion: bring to the boiling point. Pour the mixture over the meat. The liquid should cover about ¾ of the meat; turn the meat once to moisten the whole. Cover and refrigerate for about 2 days, turning the meat twice a day. Remove meat from marinade, pat it dry, drain the liquid and reserve. Measure 3 cups of the marinade and reserve the rest for the sauce.

Preheat oven to 375° F.

Put meat into a casserole with a lid, pack the chopped onions, carrots, and celery leaves around it, and pour over the 3 cups of marinade. Cover and roast in the preheated oven for about 2 hours. After 2 hours, check for doneness and, if necessary, continue baking until meat is fork tender. Do not overcook. The cooking time depends on the thickness of the cut as well as the grade of meat. Remove meat from casserole, cover with aluminum foil, and keep warm.

Drain the liquid from the casserole into a glass measuring cup. Let the fat come to the surface and drain off as much as possible. Add enough of the remaining marinade to make 3 cups of liquid. Put into a saucepan, add the crumbled ginger snaps, and beat well until crumbs are dissolved. Heat to the boiling point. Serve sauce separately. If you prefer, instead of ginger snaps use about 1 cup imported honey cake.

POACHED MEATBALLS

This dish is known to some people as Königsberger Klopse (after the city of Königsberg). It is ideal for the day before payday, as 1½ pounds of meat will serve six to eight.

THE MEATBALLS:

½ pound ground pork	2 eggs
½ pound ground beef	5 flat anchovy fillets
½ pound ground veal	½ teaspoon ground pepper
2 tablespoons butter	1 whole onion, stuck with 2 cloves
1 large onion, chopped	1 bay leaf
4 slices of firm white bread	1 teaspoon salt
4 tablespoons light cream	

6 tablespoons butter
6 tablespoons flour
4 cups poaching liquid from meat-
    balls

Juice of 2 lemons
2 tablespoons drained capers
Salt and pepper to taste
A few drops yellow food coloring

If it is difficult to find ground pork, buy a few pork chops and grind them yourself and increase the amount of ground veal. Put all the ground meat into a bowl. Melt the butter, add the chopped onion, and sauté until just wilted; do not let the onion take on color. Add onion to meat. Trim the slices of bread and moisten with the cream, crumble and add to meat. Add eggs, anchovy fillets, and pepper; mix well. Put through a meat grinder, using a coarse blade. Grind through a second time but this time using a fine blade. This fine-blade grinding is the most important step and will make for a light meatball. Divide the ground meat into 16 parts, and shape each into a ball. If you have trouble shaping the balls, dip your hands into flour before rolling them.

Into a large pot, put enough water to cover the meatballs by about 2 inches. Add the whole onion, bay leaf, and salt. Bring to a boiling point, then reduce to a simmer and add the meatballs. Do not let them come to the boiling point or they will break; keep at a simmer, watch them very carefully and do not cover. After about 20–25 minutes the meatballs will come to the surface one after the other, indicating that they are done. Remove the meatballs from the poaching liquid, cover them with a damp cloth, and mix the sauce.

Melt the butter, add the flour and blend. Add the poaching liquid and beat until smooth; add lemon juice and capers and taste for seasoning. Very carefully, add the yellow food coloring to give the sauce a light ivory color. Put the meatballs into the sauce and reheat to the simmering point. Serve with parsley potatoes.

BOILED BEEF AND HORSERADISH SAUCE

My mother used to call this "the washerwoman's dinner," and she was always horrified when I served it for a formal party. My guests were delighted, and it is an easy dinner because it does not require last-minute timing. I am extravagant and use eye round of beef because it slices so very well.

THE BEEF:

4–5 pounds eye round of beef, or use a thin cut of fresh brisket

8 carrots

1 whole onion stuck with 1 clove

8 sprigs parsley

2 chicken bouillon cubes

THE HORSERADISH SAUCE:

6 tablespoons butter or margarine

6 tablespoons flour

1 cup Half & Half

2 cups cooking stock

One or two 3-ounce jars prepared white horseradish, drained

Salt and pepper to taste

Wipe meat and let it come to room temperature. Scrape carrots, but leave whole. In a stew pot that will hold the meat easily, combine carrots, onions, parsley, and chicken bouillon cubes and add water to fill the pot about halfway. Simmer for 30 minutes, then add the meat. If meat is not well covered, add more water. Simmer for 2 hours, then test for doneness. Continue simmering until meat is fork tender. It is best to start early, as the cooking time may vary according to the quality of the meat. Leave meat and carrots in liquid while making horseradish sauce.

Melt the butter or margarine, add flour and blend. Add the Half & Half and the beef cooking stock and bring to the boiling point. Stir until smooth. Keep warm in a water bath or double boiler until ready to use. When ready to serve, drain the horseradish and add to the sauce; bring just to the boiling point, but do not boil. Boiling will cut the flavor of the horseradish. If you like a strong horseradish flavor, use the full 2 jars, less for a milder sauce. Slice meat and serve each guest meat and one whole carrot. Pass the sauce separately and accompany with boiled potatoes.

CHICKEN WITH HAM AND CHEESE

8 boneless halves broiler chicken breasts (4 whole breasts)
6 cups chicken stock, homemade (see page 68) or canned
8 slices of boiled ham
8 slices of Swiss cheese

6 tablespoons margarine or butter
½ onion, chopped very fine
½ pound mushrooms, chopped very fine
Salt and pepper to taste

Preheat oven to 350° F.

Arrange the chicken breasts in a roasting pan in a single layer. Bring the chicken stock to the boiling point, pour over the chicken, cover, and let stand for 20 minutes. Have ham and cheese at room temperature. In a frying pan, heat the margarine or butter, add the onion, and cook over low heat until the onion turns yellow. Add the mushrooms, and cook until the mushrooms get soft. Reduce heat and simmer without a cover until moisture has almost evaporated. Put the mixture into a blender and purée. Season with salt and pepper to taste. When it is serving time, remove the chicken from the broth and transfer to a baking dish. Divide the mushroom purée among the chicken breasts and spread it evenly. Put a slice of ham and a slice of cheese on top of the mushroom spread and bake for 10 minutes in the preheated oven until cheese starts to melt. Serve immediately.

CHICKEN AND MUSHROOM CASSEROLE

8 chicken quarters, either all dark,   2 teaspoons salt
    all white, or mixed   ¾ teaspoon fresh ground pepper
2 pounds fresh mushrooms   2 tablespoons chopped parsley
½ cup melted butter or margarine

Preheat oven to 350° F.

Rinse and clean the chicken parts; wash and slice the mushrooms. Put 2 tablespoons of the melted butter or margarine into the bottom of a casserole with a tight-fitting lid. Add one-third of the mushrooms and put half the chicken quarters on top; add half the remaining mushrooms, top with the rest of the chicken quarters, and finish with the last of the mushrooms. To the remaining butter or margarine, add salt and pepper and pour over the contents in the casserole. Cover and bake in the preheated oven for an hour to an hour and a half, depending upon whether the chicken quarters used were from a broiler or a fryer. Sprinkle with parsley and serve directly from the casserole.

VARIATIONS:

1) Reduce butter or margarine by half and add ½ cup sherry.

2) My friend, Emily Hammond, puts slices of Bermuda onion into the bottom of the casserole and otherwise proceeds as above.

BEEF AND CHICKEN

    2–3 pounds beef brisket
    4–6 cups vegetable stock (see page 69)
    2 broiler/fryers, 2½ pounds each, quartered
    Salt and pepper to taste

Rinse brisket and put into a stew pot; add enough vegetable stock to cover well, simmer for about 1 hour, then test for doneness. Continue cooking until meat is almost done. Rinse chicken quarters and add to brisket; bring to the boiling point and simmer for 25–30 minutes. When both meats are done, slice beef and serve some beef slices with each quarter chicken. The broth can be served on the side. If desired, cook 8 peeled carrots, 8 small peeled turnips, and 8 small peeled onions along with the beef and serve as vegetables.

MOUSSAKA

Of the many Moussaka recipes, this is the favorite version of Thalia Sophia Daratsakis Mazurek.

3 medium-sized eggplants, about 1 pound each	*One 8-ounce can tomato sauce*
	¼ teaspoon cinnamon
Salt	*½ teaspoon oregano*
2 tablespoons butter	*¼ teaspoon nutmeg*
2 onions, chopped, about 1 cup	*2 tablespoons chopped parsley*
1 clove garlic, minced	*1 teaspoon pepper*
2 pounds ground lamb	*½ cup red wine*

THE SAUCE:

6 tablespoons butter	*½ teaspoon white pepper*
6 tablespoons flour	*Olive oil for brushing the pan*
3 cups milk	*About 8 tablespoons grated*
⅛ teaspoon nutmeg	*Parmesan cheese*
½ teaspoon salt	

Preheat oven to 350° F.

Score eggplants lengthwise, at 1-inch intervals, and peel every other strip. Cut crosswise in ½-inch slices, sprinkle each slice with salt, and arrange on paper towels to absorb liquid from weeping eggplant slices. Melt the butter in a large saucepan, add the onions and garlic, and sauté until onions are soft. Add the lamb and brown lightly, breaking up the meat; add the tomato sauce, cinnamon, oregano, nutmeg, parsley, salt and pepper, and the red wine. Cook, stirring occasionally over low heat, until all moisture has evaporated. While the meat mixture is cooking, prepare the sauce.

Melt the butter, add flour and blend; add the milk and stir well to blend. Simmer over low heat until the sauce has thickened, then add nutmeg, salt, white pepper and set aside.

Pat the eggplant slices dry, brush a frying pan with olive oil, and quickly brown the eggplant slices on both sides, a few at a time, brushing the pan with oil in between. Grease a 9" X 12" X 2"-baking pan with more olive oil, arrange half the browned eggplant slices at the bottom, sprinkle lightly with Parmesan cheese, then add all the meat mixture. Top with the remaining slices of eggplant and sprinkle heavily with grated Parmesan cheese. Pour the white sauce over the whole and again sprinkle heavily with Parmesan cheese. Bake in the preheated oven for 45–60 minutes, until golden brown.

Let stand to cool for 5–10 minutes, then cut into squares and serve.

PRUNED PORK

1 pound pitted prunes   *1 teaspoon salt*
1½ cups red wine   *½ teaspoon pepper*
4–5 pounds pork loin   *Additional red wine and water*
½ teaspoon each ground ginger,
       allspice, cinnamon,
       cloves, nutmeg

Preheat oven to 350° F.

Soak the pitted prunes in 1 cup of the red wine for about a half-hour. Rinse and pat dry the meat. Cut along ribs and chine and loosen meat from bone. Insert as many prunes as will fit into the space between the bones and meat. Arrange meat in a lidded casserole just big enough to hold it and add remaining prunes and their wine. Combine all spices and seasonings with the remaining ½ cup red wine and add to meat. Check the liquid and add enough wine and water to cover the meat three-quarters of the way. Cover and roast for 2 hours in the preheated oven. Remove cover and check for doneness. Continue roasting uncovered until meat is fork tender and its internal temperature has reached 175°. Let roast stand for about a half-hour before removing from casserole. Take meat off the bones in 1 piece and slice for serving. Skim off fat from the liquid in the casserole, then serve as gravy with or without thickening. Serve prunes on the side.

POT ROAST

4 pounds bottom round roast	*3 white turnips, peeled and diced*
2 onions, chopped	*Red wine and water*
6 ribs celery, sliced	*1 bay leaf*
6 carrots, scraped and sliced	*Salt and pepper to taste*

Preheat oven to 325° F.

Select a lidded casserole that is large enough to just hold the meat. Rinse and wipe the meat and put it into the casserole. Combine all vegetables and pack them under and around the meat. Add enough red wine and water to about half cover the meat. Add the bay leaf and roast in the preheated oven for about 3 hours. Test for doneness and, if necessary, continue cooking until meat is fork tender. Some cuts take as long as 4 hours. Remove meat from casserole and put the vegetables through a food mill. Purée as much as possible, then discard the fibrous remnants. Thin out the puréed vegetables with wine to the consistency of a medium-thick gravy. Season with salt and pepper to taste. Then reheat meat in its gravy. Slice meat and serve the gravy on the side.

ROAST FILET OF BEEF

1 untrimmed beef tenderloin, 6–7 pounds
4 slices of bacon

For 8 people a beef tenderloin is cheaper than steaks, even considering that of the 6–7 pounds about 3 pounds of fat must be trimmed off.

Preheat oven to 375° F.

Holding the knife almost parallel to the meat to avoid cutting into the filet, remove all fat. When the fat is gone, remove the tendons and the meat strip that runs along the tenderloin. Be careful to remove all fat at the head of the filet—the thickest part. When all fat and skin are removed, there remains a long slender piece of meat without marble. Cover the meat with the slices of bacon (a substitute for the lardoons that used to be the classical way of preparing a filet). Roast the filet in the preheated oven for 45 minutes for rare. Using the instant meat thermometer, the internal reading should be about 110°. Remove the filet from the oven and let it stand for 10–15 minutes before slicing. By that time the internal temperature will have reached about 120°. For medium-rare, roast about 6–7 minutes longer—don't try to make it well done.

N O T E :
The tendon and the meat that have been removed can be used for

goulash or ground. Scrape the meat off the tendon and discard the tendon. The removed fat can be melted down and used as suet.

A HOLIDAY BIRD

At Thanksgiving and Christmas I like to gather together those of my friends who are unable to be with their families. All of them love to take home a bag with extra turkey for a sandwich the next day. Therefore, I always get a turkey that is much larger than the group requires. Besides that, larger turkeys are usually less expensive. As for the stuffing, I figure about one cup for each guest. This, of course, does not fill the cavity of a large bird, but there is no rule that a turkey has to be fully stuffed. Also, I do not like basting; consequently, I pick up an old idea and cover the turkey completely with strips of bacon, each one secured with toothpicks. When the turkey is ready to go into the oven it looks like a porcupine.

THE STUFFING:

6–7 eating apples

One 16-ounce package seedless
    raisins

2 cups chopped nuts (any except
    peanuts)

6–8 slices of white bread, trimmed

1 stick butter or margarine
    (4 ounces)

Peel, core, and quarter the apples, then cut into thin slices. Add the raisins and the nuts, crumble the bread and add; melt the butter and pour over the whole. Mix well. Cover and refrigerate until ready to cook the turkey.

THE TURKEY AND GRAVY:

1 turkey, about 16–20 pounds
6 cups vegetable stock (see page 69)

or

6 cups water and *1 onion stuck with 1 clove,*
1 bay leaf, 2 cups chopped celery
Salt, peper, and ground ginger
1 pound bacon
2 tablespoons cornstarch

The day before cooking the turkey, take out neck, gizzards, and liver and put all of them into a saucepan with the vegetable stock, *or* the water, onion, bay leaf, and chopped celery. Bring to the boiling point and simmer until the gizzards are tender. Strain, discard neck and vegetables, chop gizzards and liver, put into a small bowl, and cover with stock. Cool and refrigerate overnight. Also cool and refrigerate the remaining cooking liquid.

The day of the party, preheat oven to 350° F. Wash the turkey and sprinkle inside with salt, pepper, and ground ginger. Stuff the neck cavity first, because a well-rounded turkey breast is a very impressive sight. Secure the neck flap with the wings. Put the rest of the stuffing into the belly cavity and close the turkey by sticking small skewers through the skin and then tying it with string. Tie the legs together. Now arrange the strips of bacon over the whole turkey, legs and all, securing them with toothpicks. Put turkey on a rack in a roasting pan, add 1 cup of water to the roasting pan so the fat will not burn, and put the turkey into the preheated oven. Roast for about 15 minutes to the pound; however, realize that all turkeys are different and cooking times vary. The best way to find out whether the turkey is done is to pierce the spot where the leg joins the body and see whether the liquid runs clear. If it does, the turkey is done. Another indication is when the leg begins to move; in other words, the turkey is ready to shake hands. When the turkey is just beginning to get done, remove all bacon strips to brown the breast. Do not carve the turkey until it has rested for at least a half-hour. An hour is even better. And remember that while the turkey is resting, it still continues to cook.

THE GRAVY:

While the turkey is resting, skim off the fat, add about 2 cups of the reserved gizzard cooking broth or red wine to the pan, and scrape well to loosen all clinging bits. Put into a saucepan, add 2 tablespoons of cornstarch moistened with some more gizzard cooking broth, and heat. Add enough additional gizzard cooking broth to thin the gravy to the desired consistency. Add the gizzards* and taste for seasoning. If the sauce is not brown enough, add any of the caramel cooking liquids, such as Gravy Master. If a sharper gravy is desired, season with Worcestershire or soy sauce. Simmer for 10 minutes, then put the gravy into a double boiler or water bath to keep warm and reheat it at the last minute.

After the turkey has rested, slice it in the usual manner: wings off, thighs and legs off, slice for dark meat. Slice breast meat beginning at the breastbone end. This takes about a half-hour. Put all sliced meats onto platter. If you are lucky, you may have one of your guests take over the slicing while you are reheating the vegetables, cooking the green ones, heating the plates, and getting everything organized.

*NOTE:

If you like more chopped-up gizzards, add some chicken gizzards to the turkey gizzards when first cooking them.

ROAST LEG OF LAMB

Roasting a leg of lamb properly is not easy. It is not possible to give a simple formula, such as so many minutes per pound, because cooking time depends upon the shape of the leg and the degree of doneness desired. Legs of lamb come in two shapes. Long and lean, or short and plump. Obviously they will roast at different speeds, as it takes less time to heat through to the center of the long and lean.

Then there is also the complication of the degree of doneness: rare, pink, or well done. I always ask my friends how they like it. Strangely enough, some who cannot get their beef rare enough will ask for well-done lamb. Nobody ever votes for rare, so it's either pink or well done, and the majority decides. For pink lamb, roast to no more than 135°, internal temperature, and let it rest for 10–15 minutes before carving. For well done, roast to 150°, then let it rest again.

    1 leg of lamb, 6–7 pounds   *Dried thyme*
    6–8 cloves garlic (optional)   *1 cup white wine*
    Salt and pepper   *2 cups chopped onion*

Preheat oven to 350° F.

Remove fell (the glassy-looking skin) from the lamb and trim off fat. Cut garlic cloves in slivers and, with a sharp knife, cut slits in the lamb. Push garlic slivers into the slits. Mix salt, pepper, and thyme, and rub over lamb. Put lamb on a rack in a roasting pan. Put wine into a blender along with the onions, and purée. Pour the onion purée into the roasting pan. Roast for about 1 hour, then test with an instant meat thermometer. Calculate when the lamb will be done. It takes about 1 additional minute for each degree of internal temperature. When the lamb is done, remove from oven and keep warm. Pour pan drippings into a saucepan and spoon off as much fat as possible.* The gravy should be quite thick from the puréed onions, but if a thicker sauce is desired, blend some flour with melted butter and add. If a thinner sauce is desired add some wine. Reheat the sauce. Always serve lamb on hot plates.

* N O T E :
A trick to removing lamb fat, which coagulates very quickly, is to float ice cubes on top of the liquid.

WARREN KINSMAN'S MEAT LOAF CUBES

This is a moist meat loaf, very good with scalloped potatoes and a green salad or vegetable for a buffet supper.

Pam
2½ pounds lean ground beef
chuck
¼ pound ground veal
¼ pound ground pork
3 eggs
3 tablespoons butter or margarine
2 medium-sized onions, chopped,
or use one 10-ounce
package frozen chopped
onions

1 tablespoon salt
2 teaspoons pepper
Two 16-ounce cans stewed
tomatoes, or *use 2 cans*
regular tomatoes, or *2 cans*
crushed tomatoes
1 teaspoon Season All
1 teaspoon oregano
1 cup milk
½ cup dry bread crumbs

Preheat oven to 375° F.

Select a 13" x 10" x 3"-roasting pan and spray with Pam. Have the butcher grind together the beef, veal, and pork, or do it yourself. Put the meat into a bowl, beat the 3 eggs and add them to the meat. Heat the butter or margarine and sauté the chopped onions until transparent; set aside. To the meat and eggs add salt and pepper. Drain the tomatoes over the meat and chop the tomato pieces fine; do not use a blender because you want to show flecks of tomato in the meat loaf. Add the chopped tomatoes to the meat, the Season All, oregano, and finally the sautéed chopped onions. Mix well, and gradually add the milk, then work in the dry bread crumbs. This will make a soft mixture, but it should not be so soft that when cut through with a spatula it does not hold its shape. If the tomatoes were too liquid add just a bit more dry bread crumbs. Pour the whole into the prepared roasting pan and bake in the preheated oven for 1 hour and 30 minutes. Let stand for 10 minutes, then cut into cubes and serve.

CHICKEN BREASTS IN CURRY SAUCE
AND PINEAPPLE

3 cups chopped, peeled, cored apples, about 4 large
3 cups chopped onion, about 3 large
5½ cups chicken stock, home-made (see page 68) or canned
1–2 tablespoons curry powder, depending upon variety used

2 bananas
3 tablespoons peanut butter
8 halves boneless, skinless chicken breasts, cut from broilers
8 slices of pineapple, canned in its own juice

In a saucepan, combine apples, onions, 2½ cups of the chicken stock, and curry powder; bring to the boiling point, cover, and cook for about 45 minutes, until the apples and onions are soft. Remove from heat, let cool a bit, then ladle half the mixture into a blender, add a banana, and purée. Purée the second half of the liquid with the second banana, put the whole into a saucepan and, with a wire whisk, beat in the peanut butter. Reheat and put the sauce into a double boiler to keep warm until serving.

While the sauce is cooking, arrange the chicken breasts in a shallow roasting pan, bring the remaining 3 cups of stock to the boiling point, and pour over the chicken breasts. Cover and let stand for 10 minutes. Pour the stock back into a saucepan, reheat, and pour over the chicken breasts once more. Cover and let stand for 20 minutes or more.

To assemble: Warm pineapple slices in the oven, arrange on a serving platter, top with the chicken breasts, and pour over some of the curry sauce. Serve more curry sauce on the side. Any leftover curry sauce can be used with fish, eggs, or leftover meat.

ROAST VEAL SHOULDER

1 shoulder of veal, boned, about 4 pounds boned weight
1 pound sharp Cheddar cheese
6 strips of bacon
½ cup white wine

Preheat oven to 325° F.

Rub meat with a damp cloth. Cut cheese into sticks about 1½ to 2 inches long and about the diameter of a pencil. With an ice pick, punch holes in the meat and insert the slivers of cheese. Arrange bacon strips on top and secure them with toothpicks. Place the meat in a roasting pan and add the wine. Roast for 2 hours in the preheated oven; then remove the bacon strips and continue roasting for another 30 minutes to 1 hour, or until the internal temperature of the meat reaches 165°. If the liquid evaporates, add more wine as needed. Keep the meat warm for 20 minutes before slicing. Use the pan drippings as gravy, and thicken with cornstarch if desired.

ROAST SHOULDER OF PORK

1 pork shoulder, about 6 pounds   *Summer savory, ground*
Salt   *1 clove garlic, cut in half*
Pepper

Preheat oven to 300° F.

Wipe the pork shoulder with a damp cloth; combine salt, pepper, and summer savory. Rub shoulder with the split garlic clove, then rub in the mixed seasonings. If you like cracklings (for many the best part of the roast), score the skin in a diamond pattern. Roast for about 3 hours to an internal temperature of 170°. If you want a crackly skin, raise the oven temperature to 400° F. for the last 15 minutes. Baste occasionally with pan drippings. If you do not want a crackling skin, remove the skin about 30 minutes before the roasting is finished. Cut the fat end of the skin in a diamond pattern, mix ½ pound of brown sugar with 2 tablespoons of bread crumbs, moisten with lemon juice, and spread this over the roast. Raise the oven temperature to 350° F. and finish roasting. Test for doneness with an instant meat thermometer. Let the roast stand for 15–20 minutes before carving.

STUFFED CORNISH HENS

This is Kay Peer's favorite party dish.

4 Cornish hens
1 lemon, cut in half

THE STUFFING:

¼ pound chicken livers	*4 tablespoons chopped parsley*
5 tablespoons butter	*½ teaspoon ground sage*
2 tablespoons oil	*¼ teaspoon ground thyme*
4 tablespoons chopped onion	*2 cups fresh white bread crumbs*
½ pound mushrooms, sliced	*¾ cup dry white wine*
¼ pound boiled ham, chopped	
2 ounces blanched almonds, chopped	

THE GLAZE:

4 tablespoons butter or margarine
½ cup red currant jelly
¾ cup dry white wine

Preheat oven to 350° F.

Clean the hens, wash and pat dry; use gizzards and necks for other purposes, but add livers to the chicken livers for the stuffing. Rub hens inside and out with the cut lemon. Set aside to prepare stuffing.

Pick over chicken livers and trim off tendons. Heat 3 tablespoons of the butter and 1 tablespoon of the oil, add chicken livers and Cornish hen livers, and sauté for 2–3 minutes; remove from fat and chop. Put into a bowl. To the fat in the pan add the remaining 2 tablespoons of butter and 1 tablespoon oil, add the onions, and sauté until soft. Add mushrooms and ham and sauté for 1 minute. Then add almonds, parsley, sage, thyme, bread crumbs and, finally, the white wine, and cook for just ½ minute. Add the whole to the chopped livers and mix well. When cool enough to handle, stuff the hens and wrap each one in aluminum foil. Place them close together in a baking dish or roasting pan and bake in the preheated oven for 1 hour. In the meantime prepare the glaze.

Melt butter, add currant jelly, and, over low heat, melt the jelly; then add the wine and set aside. After 1 hour, unwrap the hens and brush with glaze. Continue roasting for another 20–30 minutes, glazing often. Cut hens in half and serve one half to each guest.

PARSLIED CORNISH HENS

4 Cornish hens	8 slices of bacon
1 lemon, cut in half	½–¾ cup white wine
Salt and pepper	2 teaspoons cornstarch
2 large bunches parsley	8 sprigs parsley, for garnish

Preheat oven to 350° F.

Remove liver, gizzard, and neck from hens and use for other purposes. Wash hens and pat dry, rub with lemon inside and out, then sprinkle with salt and pepper. Wash and dry parsley. Divide each bunch in half and stuff inside the hens. Arrange 2 bacon slices over each hen and secure them with toothpicks. Place the hens close together in a baking dish, add about ½ cup white wine, and roast for 1 hour. Remove bacon strips and roast for another half-hour. Remove hens from pan and add a bit more wine to the liquid in the pan. Pour the liquid into a saucepan and thicken the gravy with cornstarch. Remove parsley from hens and discard. Cut each hen in half, arrange on a platter, and garnish with fresh parsley sprigs. Serve gravy on the side.

TARRAGON CHICKEN

Many, many years ago, I tasted this dish at Marjorie Meier's farm in Maryland. She gave me the recipe, and I have served it in my home many times.

*2 fryers, each about 3½ pounds,
    cut into serving pieces
½ stick butter or margarine,
    melted (2 ounces)
1 teaspoon salt
1 teaspoon dried tarragon
¼ teaspoon garlic powder*

*⅛ teaspoon pepper
½ cup cider vinegar
2 tablespoons tarragon vinegar
½ cup chicken stock, homemade
    (see page 68) or
    canned
2 tablespoons chopped parsley*

Preheat oven to 350° F.

Wash chicken pieces, pat dry and brush with melted butter or margarine. Mix salt, tarragon, garlic powder, and pepper and sprinkle over the chicken. Arrange chicken pieces in a single layer in a roasting pan and cover with aluminum foil. Bake covered in the preheated oven for a half-hour, then uncover, add cider and tarragon vinegar, and continue baking for another 20–30 minutes, until chicken is brown and tender. Remove chicken and keep warm. To the pan juices, add the chicken stock, reheat on top of the stove, add chopped parsley, and serve as gravy.

STUFFED VEGETABLES

8 Medium-sized Tomatoes
Cut off and reserve tops, scrape out seeds, and stand upside down to drain. Fill tomatoes with a selected filling, put tops back on, and bake for 20–30 minutes in a 375° F. oven.

4 Green Peppers
Cut in half, cut off stems, remove seeds and membranes, and par-boil in salted water from 5–7 minutes. Drain, cool, and stuff halves with selected filling. Bake for 20–30 minutes in a 375° F. oven.

4 Cucumbers
Peel, cut in half, and remove seeds. Stuff with selected filling and set close together in a baking dish. Add ½ cup chicken stock and bake for 20–30 minutes in a 375° F. oven. If desired, and cucumbers are large, use only 2 cucumbers and, after baking, cut them into quarters.

FILLING: I
For 8 pepper halves or 8 medium-sized tomatoes.

1 pound ground beef	Salt and pepper to taste
1 onion, chopped	1 teaspoon oregano
2 tablespoons oil	½ cup tomato juice
2 cups cooked rice	

Combine beef, onion, and oil in a pan and sauté until onions are transparent and meat is slightly browned. Add rice, salt, pepper, and oregano, and mix.

Stuff either pepper halves or tomatoes, and moisten filling with tomato juice before baking.

FILLING: 2

For any of the 8 vegetable portions.

> ½ pound sausage meat
> 2 cups mashed potatoes
> 2 tablespoons chopped parsley

Brown sausage meat, pour off excess fat, add meat to mashed potatoes, add parsley and mix. Fill any of the vegetables and bake according to instructions.

FILLING: 3

2 tablespoons butter or margarine	4 slices of white bread
5 scallions, cut into fine rings	Salt and pepper
2 cups cooked meat, chopped fine	1 egg, beaten
(turkey, chicken, lamb, veal)	

Melt the butter, add scallion rings, and sauté for 1 minute; add meat, mix, then turn off heat. (If uncooked veal or lamb is used, cook meat until lightly browned.) Trim bread slices, crumble, moisten with water, and squeeze dry. Add to the meat mixture and taste for seasoning. Blend in the beaten egg and stuff selected vegetables.

NOTE:

Allow 2–3 varieties for each serving. Do not hesitate to vary recipes and use up leftover meat and vegetables. For example, leftover lima beans, peas, or corn make ideal additions to the sausage recipe, if you cut down on the amount of mashed potatoes.

ED COTA'S SPAGHETTI SAUCE

Ed is a spaghetti fiend, and his spaghetti sauce is very good and very simple; it only takes 2 hours' cooking time.

1 tablespoon oil
1¼ pounds chopped lean beef
    chuck
6 links hot Italian pork sausage
6 links sweet Italian pork sausage
1 bunch parsley
3 medium-sized onions, chopped
3 medium-sized carrots, scraped
    and chopped
3 ribs of celery, chopped
1 green pepper, trimmed and
    chopped

2 cloves garlic, peeled and
    chopped
1 cup red wine
1 teaspoon oregano
1 tablespoon mint flakes
One 28-ounce can peeled Italian
    tomatoes
One 15-ounce can tomato sauce
Two 6-ounce cans tomato paste
One 10-ounce can tomato soup

Put the tablespoon of oil into a large stew pot and heat; add the chopped beef. Remove the meat from the Italian sausages and add to the beef; mix the whole well, brown lightly, and set aside. Rinse the bunch of parsley. In a blender, purée the chopped vegetables and parsley, using either the red wine or the liquid drained from the tomatoes to moisten. Add the puréed vegetables to the browned meat; add oregano, mint flakes, tomatoes, tomato sauce, tomato paste, and tomato soup. Stir well, and simmer for 2 hours. This makes 4 quarts of spaghetti sauce that is on the hot side. If you like it milder, use 12 sweet Italian sausages and eliminate the hot. Any leftover sauce can be frozen. This will be enough sauce for at least 2 pounds of pasta.

VEGETABLES

BAKED POTATOES

8 *Idaho potatoes*	*½ teaspoon salt*
1 cup cottage cheese	*¼ onion*
½ cup plain yoghurt	

Preheat oven to 450° F.

Scrub potatoes and prick them all over with a fork. Arrange on a baking sheet and bake for 35–40 minutes, or until done. While potatoes are baking, prepare the following dressing: Combine cottage cheese and yoghurt in a blender and purée until very smooth. Add salt and the onion in bits; purée some more. Refrigerate until ready to serve.

VARIATION:
Omit onion and add chives after puréeing the cottage cheese and yoghurt.

RISI BISI

4 tablespoons butter or margarine   One 10-ounce package frozen
¾ cup chopped onion   peas, cooked according
1¼ cup uncooked regular rice   to package instructions
2¾ cups hot water

In a large frying pan, melt the butter or margarine, add onions, and sauté until onions begin to yellow. Wash rice and add to the onions, together with 2 cups of the hot water. Cook over low heat, stirring frequently, until liquid has been absorbed and rice begins to get soft. Add cooked peas and the remaining water. Continue cooking until rice is done and all the liquid has been absorbed.

FRESH ASPARAGUS

40 spears of asparagus, preferably   1 teaspoon salt
    medium-thick or thick, al-   1 lemon
    lowing 5 stalks per person   1 cup melted butter

Wash asparagus and trim off hard ends; put ends into a saucepan and cover with water; add salt. Press out lemon, reserve juice, and add pressed-out shells to the asparagus ends. Simmer for 30–40 minutes. Put the trimmed asparagus spears in water and let soak. After 15 minutes, test the water for sand particles. If there is no sand, remove the asparagus and wrap in cheesecloth. If asparagus are sandy, scrub them well before wrapping. Place the wrapped asparagus into a pot that holds them easily. Pour the liquid from the asparagus ends over the tips; if needed, add more water to cover. Simmer for 15–20 minutes for medium-sized asparagus, longer for thick ones. Test with a fork for doneness. Drain off some of the water from the asparagus, then arrange them on a serving platter. Remove the cheesecloth and drain off any remaining water. To the melted butter add the reserved lemon juice and pour over asparagus before serving.

NOTE:
Save cooking liquid and asparagus ends for Asparagus Soup (see page 135).

BEETS AND ONIONS

Two 16-ounce cans sliced beets
3 large onions
½ cup vinegar
4 tablespoons sugar

Drain beet juice into a saucepan; reserve sliced beets. Slice onions and cut slices into thirds. Add onions to beet juice along with vinegar and sugar. Simmer until onions are soft, then add sliced beets. Bring back to the boiling point and drain before serving.

GREEN BEANS AND BAMBOO SHOOTS

Two 10-ounce packages frozen French-cut green beans
One 8-ounce can bamboo shoots
2 tablespoons butter

Cook the frozen beans according to package instructions until almost tender. Add the bamboo shoots and continue cooking until beans are done. Drain the whole and blend in the butter. Serve immediately.

SAUERKRAUT WITH PINEAPPLE

3 pounds sauerkraut
One 18-ounce can unsweetened pineapple juice
Two 8-ounce cans unsweetened pineapple chunks

Rinse sauerkraut very well and press dry; put it into a saucepan and add unsweetened pineapple juice. Drain the juice from the pineapple chunks and add to the sauerkraut. Add enough water to cover the sauerkraut well. Simmer at low heat for about 1½–2 hours. Just before serving, drain sauerkraut, but reserve liquid in case of leftovers. Add the pineapple chunks to the sauerkraut, mix well, and serve.

FANCY MIXED VEGETABLES

These are known in Europe as *Leipziger Allerlei* and are sold packaged in glass jars at a fancy price. They usually contain the dark mushrooms called morrels which lend a beautiful contrast to the other vegetables; however, the dish can be prepared without them.

2 cups cauliflowerettes, either fresh or frozen, about one 10-ounce package, frozen
2 cups whole young carrots, canned or frozen
1 cup fresh green peas, or half a 10-ounce package frozen tiny peas
One 4-ounce can button mushrooms
One 10-ounce package frozen asparagus tips
½ cup lima beans (optional)
½ cup green beans (optional)
6 tablespoons butter or margarine
3 tablespoons flour
1½ cups combined vegetable cooking liquid
1 tablespoon lemon juice
Salt and pepper to taste

Cook all the vegetables separately. If using frozen, follow package instructions. Drain vegetables. Reserve and combine the cooking liquids and put all vegetables together in a pot. Melt the butter or margarine, blend in flour and add 1½ cups of the reserved cooking liquid. Add lemon juice and simmer, stirring until sauce is thickened. Season with salt and pepper to taste. Pour the sauce over the vegetables and reheat before serving.

CAULIFLOWER CASSEROLE

1 medium-sized head cauliflower, or two 10-ounce packages frozen cauliflower
½ teaspoon nutmeg
2 tablespoons butter or margarine

2 tablespoons flour
1 cup milk or Half & Half
Bread crumbs
1 tablespoon melted butter or margarine

Preheat oven to 350° F.

Break cauliflower into flowerettes and cook until soft, about 15–20 minutes, in just enough water to cover, with ½ teaspoon nutmeg. Or cook frozen cauliflower according to package instructions with nutmeg added. Drain and reserve cooking liquid. Melt the butter or margarine, blend in flour and add 1 cup of the cooking liquid. Stir well to blend, then add 1 cup milk or Half & Half and simmer until sauce thickens; if necessary, add a bit more milk. Combine with cooked cauliflower and pour into a 1½–2-quart baking dish. Sprinkle with bread crumbs and dribble melted butter or margarine on top. Bake in the preheated oven for about 30 minutes.

SPINACH PIE

Two 10-ounce packages frozen   *7 medium eggs*
chopped spinach   *1½ cups Half & Half*
2 tablespoons vinegar   *Butter for pan*
½ teaspoon nutmeg

Preheat oven to 350° F.

Cook spinach according to package instructions, but add vinegar and nutmeg. When well done, drain spinach and press lightly to squeeze out surplus liquid. In a bowl, beat eggs slightly, add Half & Half and the drained chopped spinach. Butter a 10-inch pie pan, pour the spinach mixture into it, and bake in the preheated oven for 40–45 minutes, until the pie is set in the center. Turn off oven and let pie rest for 5 more minutes. Cut into 8 wedges like a regular pie and serve.

BAY LEAF POTATOES

8 medium-sized potatoes, about 2 pounds in all
Water
2 bay leaves
1 teaspoon salt

½ stick butter (2 ounces)
1 tablespoon lemon juice
2 tablespoons chopped parsley
    or
3 tablespoons butter
3 tablespoons flour
1 cup milk
½ cup light cream

Wash, peel potatoes, and quarter—slice if you want to make béchamel potatoes. Cover potatoes with water, add bay leaves, and salt and simmer until soft, about 20 minutes. Drain well, then return to heat. Dry the potatoes by heating over a very low flame, shaking constantly. For parslied bay leaf potatoes: Melt the ½ stick butter, add lemon juice, and pour over potatoes. Sprinkle with chopped parsley, mix, and serve. For béchamel potatoes: Melt the 3 tablespoons butter, add flour and stir until smooth. Add milk and cream and cook, stirring, until sauce thickens. Pour sauce over sliced potatoes and serve.

MACARONI AND CHEESE

This is Margaret O'Connor's special macaroni and cheese dish. The macaroni is not soupy, but each piece is nicely coated with cheese.

1 pound elbow macaroni	*5 cups milk*
6 tablespoons melted butter	*4 cups grated extra-sharp*
4 tablespoons flour	*Cheddar cheese*
1 teaspoon salt	*1 tablespoon paprika*
½ teaspoon pepper	*Butter*

Preheat oven to 350° F.

Cook macaroni in plenty of salted water until just done. Drain and rinse with cold water. Combine the melted butter with the flour; add salt and pepper and the 5 cups of milk. Stir until smooth, then bring to the boiling point to thicken slightly. Add the cheese, and mix until cheese is melted. Put the macaroni into a baking dish, cover with the cheese sauce, and mix well. Sprinkle with paprika and dot with butter. Bake in the preheated oven for 35–40 minutes, until bubbly.

JANSSON'S TEMPTATION MA FACON

This is Emily Richards' version of the Swedish classic.

2 yellow onions, chopped	7 baking potatoes
2 tablespoons butter	White pepper
1 tablespoon oil	Two 2-ounce cans flat anchovy fillets
1 cup heavy cream	2 tablespoons fine dry bread crumbs
½ cup milk	2 tablespoons butter

Preheat oven to 325° F.

Sauté chopped onions in butter and oil until they are soft and transparent, but do not brown. Combine cream and milk in a large saucepan and heat until lukewarm. Peel and wash potatoes and grate on the coarse side of a 4-sided household grater. Put shredded potatoes into the lukewarm cream and milk, and stir well to make sure all potato pieces are coated with liquid. This will prevent discoloring. Butter a 1½–2-quart baking dish. With a slotted spoon lift and drain about one-third of the grated potatoes and spread on the bottom of the baking dish. Put half the sautéed onions on top of the potatoes and sprinkle with a little bit of white pepper. Drain 1 can of anchovy fillets and arrange them on top of the onions. Follow with another third of the potatoes, then the rest of the onions, and the second can of drained anchovies. Sprinkle with a bit of pepper. Top with the remaining third of the potatoes. Pour the cream and milk from the potatoes over the whole and make sure that the liquid reaches to just below the top; if not, add more milk. Sprinkle the top with bread crumbs and dot with butter. Bake in the preheated oven for about 40 minutes, until potatoes are tender and the top is nicely browned. Allow to stand for 10–15 minutes before serving.

PART THREE

SALADS

RED WHITE AND GREEN SALAD

1 bunch watercress, or 2 heads   *1 medium-sized white turnip,*
   Bibb lettuce, washed   *peeled and shredded*
   and dried   *(about 1 cup)*
4 tablespoons olive oil   *¾ tablespoon wine vinegar*
1 large carrot, scraped and grated   *Salt and pepper to taste*
   coarse (about 1 cup)

Cut off heavy stems from watercress, wash, and spin dry. Put into a bowl, add 3 tablespoons of the olive oil, and mix well so all leaves are coated. Put shredded vegetables on top of watercress and refrigerate. Just before serving blend the remaining tablespoon of oil with the wine vinegar, add salt and pepper, blend, and pour over salad. Mix well.

HOT POTATO SALAD

3 pounds potatoes
8 slices of lean bacon
1 cup chopped onion
4 tablespoons wine vinegar

4 tablespoons chicken stock, homemade
(see page 68) or canned
½ teaspoon pepper

Prepare this in the afternoon.

Boil potatoes in water until just done; drain, cool a bit, then peel and slice. While potatoes are cooking, fry the bacon until crisp, remove from fat, cool, and crumble. Put potatoes into a bowl and add crumbled bacon. To bacon fat in pan add chopped onion and sauté until just transparent. Add vinegar, chicken stock, and pepper and bring to the boiling point. Pour over potatoes and mix. Do not refrigerate; serve lukewarm.

HOT CAULIFLOWER SALAD

This is best in late summer when fresh young cauliflower is on the market.

1 large head cauliflower
¼ teaspoon nutmeg
6 slices of lean bacon

2 tablespoons oil
2 tablespoons wine vinegar
Salt and pepper to taste

Prepare this in the afternoon.

Rinse cauliflower and trim off leaves and stem as far as possible without losing flowerettes. Drop into boiling water, add nutmeg, and cook for about 25 minutes. Do not overcook. While cauliflower is cooking fry the bacon until crisp. Remove the slices, drain, and crumble. Combine 2 tablespoons of the bacon fat with 2 tablespoons of oil and the vinegar, add salt and pepper, and beat until fluffy. When cauliflower is done, remove from water and drain. Place in a bowl, sprinkle with crumbled bacon, and pour on the dressing. After 15 minutes, drain off dressing and pour it on again. Repeat 3 or 4 times. Do not refrigerate. To serve, cut cauliflower into 8 wedges and serve as a salad course, either before or after the main dish.

A PRETTY SALAD PLATTER

1 large or 2 small bunches watercress *16 tablespoons Cottage Cheese*
32 cherry tomatoes *Dressing (see page*
1 large cucumber *186)*
A bunch of radishes

Wash watercress, cut off stems, and dry. Cut the tomatoes in half. Peel the cucumber, cut in half, and remove seeds. Cut ends off cucumber halves then cut each half into 4 equal pieces leaving 8 small troughs. Wash and trim the radishes and chop in a blender, a few at a time. To assemble, arrange a ring of watercress leaves around the edges of 8 salad plates, put 8 cherry tomato halves in a ring inside the watercress. Put 2 tablespoons of cottage cheese dressing in the center, fill the cucumber troughs with the chopped radishes, and put on top of the dressing. Refrigerate before serving.

CUCUMBER SALAD

3 large or 4 small cucumbers *3 tablespoons chopped fresh dill*
2 teaspoons salt *8 large lettuce leaves*
2 tablespoons wine vinegar
1½ cups Cottage Cheese Dressing
  (see page 186)

Prepare this in the morning.

Peel cucumbers, cut in half, and remove seeds. Slice them very thin and put into a bowl. Sprinkle with salt and wine vinegar and let stand for 30–40 minutes. Put in a sieve to drain for about 15 minutes. Return to bowl and add cottage cheese dressing and 2 tablespoons of the chopped dill leaves. To serve, arrange on lettuce leaves and sprinkle with remaining chopped dill.

ZUCCHINI SALAD

6 small zucchini
4 scallions, trimmed
French Dressing (see page 186)

Scrub zucchini and drop into boiling water, bring back to the boiling point, and drain. Cool. Cut zucchini lengthwise into quarters, then cut each again in half so that each strip is about as thick as a pencil. Then cut the strips in half crosswise and put them into a bowl. Wash and trim the scallions and snip into fine rings. Add to the zucchini and pour on just enough French dressing to moisten well. Refrigerate before serving.

TOMATO AND WATERCRESS SALAD PLATE

4 tomatoes
A bunch of watercress
2 cups creamed cottage cheese

2 tablespoons drained prepared white
horseradish
Salt and pepper to taste

Wash and skin tomatoes. Slice tomatoes and arrange, overlapping, in the centers of 8 salad plates. Cut off stems of watercress, wash, and dry. Divide among the salad plates and arrange around the tomato slices. To the creamed cottage cheese, add drained horseradish, salt and pepper. Spoon a ribbon of cottage cheese over the tomato slices. Refrigerate before serving.

BELGIAN ENDIVE AND BLUE CHEESE

6 Belgian endives
4 ounces blue cheese
French Dressing (see page 186)

Trim endives and cut into bite-size pieces. Wash and dry, and put into a bowl. Crumble cheese and add to endives. Pour on just enough French dressing to moisten all. Refrigerate before serving.

CHINESE PEA PODS SALAD

Two 10-ounce packages frozen Chinese pea pods
French Dressing (see page 186)
4 tomatoes

Cook pea pods according to package instructions; drain and, while still hot, pour on French dressing. Refrigerate. Skin tomatoes, cut off 8 thick slices (use leftovers for other purposes), and arrange pea pods on 8 salad plates. Remove pulp from tomato slices and cut through the rim in one spot. Arrange the tomato ribbons over the pea pods.

THE TENDEREST SALAD

This is a salad for delicate stomachs. It is made from the inner leaves of the greens, so it is all yellow. In Europe, where this is quite popular, sugar is served on the side.

3–4 heads Boston lettuce
2 heads romaine
½ cup sour cream
2 tablespoons heavy cream

Strip the heads of lettuce of their coarse outer leaves (use the discarded parts for vegetable stock). Wash the inner leaves and dry them; break into bite-sized pieces and put into a bowl. Dilute sour cream with heavy cream and pour over. Toss and arrange on salad plates. Refrigerate before serving.

FRENCH DRESSING

1 cup olive oil or salad oil   *¼ teaspoon pepper*
⅓ cup wine vinegar   *⅛ teaspoon dry mustard*
¼ teaspoon salt

Combine all the ingredients and whip together, then refrigerate.

MAKES ABOUT 1½ CUPS.

COTTAGE CHEESE DRESSING

½ cup mayonnaise   *1 slice of onion, cut into quarters*
1 cup cottage cheese   *¼ teaspoon dried tarragon*
3 tablespoons lemon juice   *1 teaspoon salt*
1 teaspoon dry mustard   *½ teaspoon pepper*

Combine all the ingredients in a blender and purée until very smooth. Refrigerate before using.

MAKES ABOUT 2 CUPS.

DESSERTS

RASPBERRY TAPIOCA PUDDING

Two 10-ounce packages frozen raspberries
3 tablespoons Minute Tapioca
Heavy cream (optional)

Defrost berries and drain; keep berries whole. To drained juice, add enough water to make 2 cups of liquid. Put into a saucepan, add tapioca, and let mixture stand for 5 minutes. Simmer for 3–4 minutes, stirring constantly. When thickened, remove from heat and add berries. Refrigerate. Serve with either whipped or fluid heavy cream.

HONEYED APPLE PIE

3 apples, Granny Smith or Rome	*White wine, apple juice, or water*
4 tablespoons honey	*1 envelope plain gelatin*
1 teaspoon cinnamon	

Preheat oven to 350° F.

Peel, core, and quarter apples. Cut each quarter into 4–5 pieces. Arrange in an 8-inch pan, standing up a bit. Dribble honey over the apples and dust with cinnamon. Cover with aluminum foil and bake for ¾–1 hour, until apples are soft. Cool a bit, then drain juice from pie. Measure juice and add enough white wine, apple juice, or water to make 1 cup. Put into a small saucepan, sprinkle gelatin over the liquid, and heat gently, stirring constantly, until gelatin is dissolved. Pour over apples in pie pan and refrigerate until set. Cut like any other pie, but loosen edge around rim before slicing. Serve with Sauce for Fruits (see page 118).

A VERY RICH CHOCOLATE DESSERT

1 cup milk	*2 tablespoons rum*
6 ounces chocolate chips	*½ pint heavy cream*
3 tablespoons sugar	*½ cup ground nuts (any except peanuts)*
1 egg	

Heat the cup of milk to the boiling point. Put the chocolate chips, 1 tablespoon of the sugar, the egg, and rum into a blender, add the boiling milk, and process for about 1 minute at low speed. Pour liquid into a bowl and refrigerate for about a half-hour. Beat the heavy cream until stiff, gradually adding the remaining 2 tablespoons of sugar. Add the ground nuts to the whipped cream. Combine with the chocolate mixture and pour into a serving bowl. Refrigerate for a few hours or overnight.

APPLE CRUMB WITH ORANGE

There are many recipes for apple crumb, but the special touch in this one is the grated orange rind in the crumbs.

1 orange	*½ cup sugar*
7 medium-sized apples	*¾ teaspoon ground cinnamon*
Butter for baking dish	

THE CRUMBS:

1 cup flour	*8 tablespoons butter*
¾ cup sugar	*Reserved orange peel*
½ teaspoon salt	

Preheat oven to 375° F.

Grate the peel from the orange and set aside; press out orange juice. Peel apples, cut into quarters, remove core, and cut into eighths. Butter a 7″ x 9″-baking dish with a rim. Arrange apple slices in the baking dish and pour on the orange juice. Blend the ½ cup sugar with the cinnamon and sprinkle over the apples. Combine all the crumb ingredients and add the grated orange peel. Press this mixture into crumbs and sprinkle over the apples. Bake for 45 minutes in the preheated oven. Serve with fluid light cream or whipped heavy cream. Ice cream would be suitable, too.

CHOCOLATE PIE

3 large egg whites
½ teaspoon cream of tartar
¾ cup sugar
1 cup pecans or walnuts, grated fine

2 ounces (2 squares) semisweet chocolate, grated
1 tablespoon melted margarine
One 4-ounce package instant chocolate pudding powder
2 tablespoons dry instant coffee

Preheat oven to 350° F.

Beat egg whites until stiff, adding cream of tartar and sugar 1 tablespoon at a time. When stiff, fold in ¾ cup of the nuts and the chocolate. Brush a 10-inch pie pan with the melted margarine, then sprinkle heavily with the reserved ¼ cup nuts. Pile the egg white/sugar/nut/chocolate mixture into the pie pan, smooth it out, and bake for 30–35 minutes in the preheated oven. Remove from oven and let cool. Prepare chocolate pudding according to package instructions but add 2 tablespoons instant coffee. Cover top of pudding with waxed paper to prevent skin from forming. When cool, pile into the meringue pie shell. Serve like any other pie, but loosen edges around the rim before slicing. The grated nuts will prevent the meringue from sticking to the pan.

FRUITS AND CHEESE

This is, of course, the classic French finish to dinner, but don't serve cheese with your cocktails if you plan this as dessert. I try to limit the choice to three fruits and three kinds of cheese. I have found the following the most popular:

Apples and sharp Cheddar
Grapes with a soft cream-type cheese
Pears with Roquefort

Melon sections with Gouda
Tangerine sections and a nutty Emmenthaler
Orange sections and feta

RICE CREAM WITH FRUITS

½ cup uncooked rice	4 tablespoons sugar
1 cup water	2 teaspoons vanilla extract
2 cups milk	8 canned peach halves, drained, or 16
½ cup butter or margarine	apricot halves, drained

Combine rice, water, milk, butter or margarine, and sugar in a sauce-pan; bring to the boiling point, then simmer over low heat until rice is very, very soft and the whole looks like moist mush. Cool a bit, then purée in a blender until smooth and the consistency of very heavy cream. Pour into a bowl and add vanilla extract. Refrigerate. Divide among 8 dessert dishes and top each serving with a peach half or 2 apricot halves.

MIXED FRUIT SALAD

Any fresh, frozen, or canned fruit can be used in a fruit salad. If you plan to use apples, peaches or pears, always include a citrus fruit to prevent darkening of the others. A very nice combination is a piece of Cranshaw melon, diced, a piece of Persian melon, diced, a package of frozen raspberries, one of frozen strawberries, seedless grapes, and a can of papaya, diced. To any fruit salad, liqueurs such as kirsch, Grand Marnier, or brandy can be added. You might also drain all canned and frozen fruits and dissolve one package of plain gelatin in

3 cups of liquid. This will not make an aspic, it only will thicken the liquid.

Allow about one cup of salad per serving.

FRESH FRUIT PLATTER

Jean Thackrey served this as dessert at a dinner party and it was stunning.

Use all seasonal fresh fruits and arrange them in rows on a large platter. That evening, it was a row of watermelon pieces cut off the rind and seeded. A row of blueberries, a row of strawberries, a row of sliced peaches, a row of bananas, and a row of apricot halves. Also suitable would be any of the other melons, grapes, orange sections, tangerine sections, sliced nectarines, and plum halves. Serve each guest a few pieces of each fruit.

BRANDIED CHOCOLATE PUDDING

3 ounces unsweetened chocolate	*11 tablespoons sugar*
¼ cup water	*½ teaspoon salt*
4 tablespoons cornstarch	*2 ounces brandy*
2 cups milk	*1 cup heavy cream*
1½ tablespoons dry instant coffee	*½ teaspoon vanilla extract*

In a quart-sized pan, melt chocolate in ¼ cup water over low heat. Blend the 4 tablespoons cornstarch with ½ cup of the milk. Add the remaining milk to the melted chocolate, then add instant coffee, 8 tablespoons of the sugar, and salt. Bring close to the boiling point, then add the blended cornstarch and simmer until thickened. Remove from heat, cool a bit, and add brandy. Blend, cover surface with waxed paper, and refrigerate. Beat heavy cream, gradually adding the remaining 3 tablespoons of sugar and the vanilla extract. Fold into the chilled chocolate pudding and put into a serving bowl or divide among individual dessert dishes.

EGG BATTER PANCAKES

These are the Middle European cousin of the French crêpes. The batter used is about the same, only these are thicker than the tissue-thin crêpes. In Vienna they are called *Palatschinken*. In the various German regions they are either *Pfannkuchen* or *Eierkuchen*. If you have a favorite crêpe batter recipe, use it, only add a bit more batter to the pan for each crêpe. For the following hot dessert, I make two pancakes for each serving in a 5½-inch cast-iron pan and fill them with a mixture of apricot jam and apricot butter. The pancakes are made ahead, filled, rolled, and put into a baking dish. As soon as the oven is free, and while dinner is being served, the pancakes are reheated in a 225° F. oven.

MAKES ENOUGH EGG BATTER FOR ABOUT 16 5½-INCH PANCAKES

1½ cups flour	*Butter for pan*
¼ teaspoon salt	*8 tablespoons apricot jam*
4 eggs, beaten	*8 tablespoons apricot butter*
2 cups milk	*¼ cup superfine granulated sugar*
2 tablespoons melted butter	*¼ cup or more rum*

Combine flour and salt. Beat eggs with milk and butter, gradually add flour, and beat together lightly. Let stand for at least 1 hour. Butter the pan and add about 1½–2 tablespoons of batter. Rotate quickly and fry on one side. Turn and brown for a few seconds on the other side, set aside, and make the remaining 15 pancakes. Mix together the apricot jam and apricot butter and fill each pancake. Roll up and arrange in a single layer in a baking dish. When dinner is ready to be served, sprinkle sugar and rum over the pancakes and place in a 225° F. oven. By the time the main course is finished, the pancakes will be hot.

CRANBERRY BANANA DESSERT

1 pound fresh cranberries   *3 cups sugar*
½ cup sweet vermouth   *3 bananas*
½ cup dry vermouth   *1 cup sour cream*
¼ cup water

Combine cranberries, sweet and dry vermouths, water, and sugar in a large saucepan. Cook over high heat, stirring constantly, until all berries have popped, about 10 minutes. Cool a bit, then purée in a blender in 2 stages, adding bananas and puréeing them, too. Pour into a bowl and beat in the sour cream. Refrigerate and divide among 8 dessert dishes.

BAKED APPLE IN AN ENVELOPE

8 baking apples   *4 tablespoons sugar*
4 tablespoons melted butter   *8 squares of aluminum foil*
5 tablespoons raisins   *4–6 tablespoons rum*

Preheat oven to 400° F.

Wash and core apples; combine melted butter, raisins, and sugar and fill the apple cavities with this mixture. Butter the aluminum squares and set filled apples on the buttered side. Sprinkle rum over apples and wrap in the foil. Set on a cookie sheet and bake for 20 minutes in the preheated oven. Serve in the wrapper with heavy cream on the side, if desired.

APPLE CUSTARD A LA JANE NICKERSON

The model for this recipe is Jane Nickerson's famous corn pudding, as described in her Florida Cook Book. It is made of freshly grated corn, custard, and suitable seasonings. Instead of corn, I used sliced apples.

2½ cups peeled, cored, and sliced apples *¾ cup light cream*
Butter for pan *1 cup brown sugar*
3 eggs

Preheat oven to 325° F.

The peeled, cored, and quartered apples can be sliced on a household grater, using the side with 3 wide slots. Put the sliced apples into a buttered 9-inch pie pan. Beat the eggs, add cream and brown sugar, and blend well. Pour over apples, and bake in the preheated oven until the center is set, about 30–45 minutes, depending upon the amount of moisture in the apples. Chill before serving like a regular pie.

VARIATION:
Fry sliced apples in about 3 tablespoons of butter, until they begin to get soft, then proceed as above. I submitted both versions to the Recipe Debating Society, and the verdict was a tie.

INDEX

Bamboo shoots, green beans and,
  175
Banana:
  cranberry dessert, 194
  curry sauce, lamb patties in, 34
  salad medley with, 41
Bass, stuffed, 137
Bay leaf, potatoes and, 178
Beans:
  green:
    bamboo shoots and, 175
    cucumber salad and, 42
    salad, 103
    tomato sauce and, 38
  lima, tomatoes and, 39
  salad with mushrooms, 104
  soup, 65
  soup, black, 10
  sweet and sour, carrots and, 97
Beef, 31–32, 71–74, 149–153, 158–
  159, 170–172
  balls, nutty, 32
  boiled, and horseradish sauce, 153
  brisket with chicken, 155
  cabbage stuffed with, 83
  corned, and cabbage, 84
  loaf, 31, 149
  pizza, 31
  pot roast, 158
  roast filet, 159
  rouladen, 82
  sauerbraten, 150
  short ribs, baked, 82
  steak, Swiss, 86

stew:
  with beer, 78
  Julia's Puerto Rican, 74
  with kidneys, 79
  with potatoes, 72
  stock, 69
  Szegediner Gulyas, 73
  tongue, smoked, 80
  Zrazi, 89
Beer, beef stewed in, 78
Beets:
  Harvard, 101
  onions and, 175
Berries, whipped cream and gelatin
  with, 111
Black bean soup, 10
Blue cheese:
  bites, 125
  endive and, 185
Bluefish:
  baked, 142
  filet, baked, 20
Brandy, 192
Broccoli, baked, 36

Cabbage:
  baked, 97
  corned beef and, 84
  red, and ham, 26
  stuffed, 83
Cake:
  cheese, 117
  fruits and, 49
  lady fingers, 50

Capers, veal patties and, 33
Caraway seed, 78
Carrots:
    gingered, 94
    nut spread, 59
    salad, with onions, 40
    salad, with peas, 104
    soup, cream, 63
    sweet and sour, beans and, 97
Casseroles:
    cauliflower, 177
    chicken and mushroom, 155
    eggplant, 100
    Jansson's Temptation, 180
    pork and rice, 88
    sweet potato, 37, 99
Cauliflower:
    casserole, 177
    cherry tomatoes and, 37
    salad, hot, 182
Celery soup, nutty, cream of, 9
Cheese (see also Cream cheese):
    cake, 117
    chicken, ham and, 154
    Liptauer, 58
    macaroni and, 179
    sandwiches, ham and, 124
    soup, 134
Cherries:
    pink, 48
    whipped cream and gelatin with,
        111
Chicken, 22–26
    beef brisket and, 155

breast:
    in curry sauce and pineapple,
        165
    with horseradish sauce, 22
    with mushrooms, 26
    with olives, 56
    in tarragon sauce, 25
    with tomato sauce and cheese,
        24
casserole with mushrooms, 155
Chinese, 23
curried, 77
fricassee, 85
ham, cheese and, 154
ham pot pie, 27
legs, baked, 24
liver pâté, 61
liver pie, 126
soup, 133
soup with anchovy custard, 133
stock, 68
tarragon, 169
Chinese:
    chicken, 23
    pea pod salad, 185
Chocolate:
    dessert, 188
    ice cream with crème de menthe,
        51
    ice cream with vanilla sauce, 48
    pie, 190
    pudding, brandied, 191
Chowder, fish, 9

Rhubarb:
  pudding, 108
  and strawberry pie, 115
  tapioca pudding, 109
Rice:
  cream with fruits, 191
  mushrooms and, 99
  and pork casserole, 88
  pudding, baked, 116
  Risi Bisi, 174
  salad, 102
  and tomato soup, 130
Rouladen, 82

Salad dressings, 45, 186
  cottage cheese, 186
  French, 186
  lemon French, 45
  mayonnaise and yoghurt, 45
Salads, 40–44, 102–107, 181–186
  artichoke hearts, 41
  asparagus, 103
  asparagus mousse, 107
  beans and mushrooms, 104
  Belgian endive and blue cheese,
    185
  Belgian endive, tomato and
    watercress, 44
  carrot and onion, 40
  cauliflower, hot, 182
  Chinese pea pods, 185
  coleslaw, 102
  cucumber, 183
  cucumber with tomatoes, 44

fancy medley, 41
fruit, hasty, 47
fruit, mixed, 191
green bean, 103
green bean and cucumber, 42
hearts of palm and watercress, 43
jellied cucumber with green
    sauce, 106
Mexican, 43
onion, 105
orange, grapefruit and endive, 41
pea pod, Chinese, 185
peas and carrots, 105
platter, 183
potato, hot, 182
red, white and green, 181
rice, 102
tenderest, 185
tomato sandwich, 42
tomato and watercress, 184
vegetable, 104
zucchini, 184
Salmon:
  poached, 138
  smoked, and cream cheese sand-
    wiches, 122
  steak, baked, 16
Sandwiches:
  cream cheese:
    olives and nuts, 124
    onions and capers, 124
    and radish, 122
    and smoked salmon, 122
  ham and cheese, 124

Irma Rhode

Born and educated in Berlin, Irma Rhode is a long-time resident of New York City. In the more than forty years that she has been a "food professional," Miss Rhode has worked, cooked, written or vacationed in all parts of the United States. *Practical Entertaining* is her second cookbook.